Elections

VOTE

Authors

Christi E. Sorrell, M.A.Ed.
Kathy Kopp, M.S.Ed.

SHELL EDUCATION

Publishing Credits

Dona Herweck Rice, *Editor-in-Chief*; Robin Erickson, *Production Director*;
Lee Aucoin, *Creative Director*; Timothy J. Bradley, *Illustration Manager*;
Sara Johnson, M.S.Ed, *Senior Editor*; Evelyn Garcia, *Associate Education Editor*;
Stephanie Reid, *Cover Designer*; Corinne Burton, M.A.Ed., *Publisher*

Image Credits
p.60 Library of Congress [LC-DIG-ggbain-02860];
p.103 Library of Congress [LC-DIG-ppmsca=08504]; p.129 John Harvey/flicker.com;
p.151 Library of Congress LC-USZ62-14831];Story page illustrations Chad Thompson;
all other images: Shutterstock.com

© 2004 Mid-continent Research for Education and Learning (McREL)
© 2007 Teachers of English to Speakers of Other Languages, Inc. (TESOL)

Shell Education
5301 Oceanus Drive
Huntington Beach, CA 92649-1030
http://www.shelleducation.com
ISBN 978-1-4258-0913-3
©2012 Shell Educational Publishing, Inc.

Table of Contents

Introduction

Unit 1: Introduction to the Process

Unit 2: Getting on the Ballot

Unit 3: The Campaign Trail

Unit 4: After the Election

Appendices

The Importance of Civic Education

"Young people must learn how to participate in a democracy."
—*Constitutional Rights Foundation* 2000

It is the responsibility of those living in the United States to understand how civics relates to them. By being able to participate in a democracy, citizens can affect the nation and its well-being. Therefore, it is necessary for students to learn and understand civics. The National Council for the Social Studies (1994) states that "social studies programs should include experiences that provide for the study of the ideals, principles, and practices of citizenship in a democratic republic." By learning civics, students can be committed to addressing social and government issues in a constructive way. However, in order to do this, students must understand the country and communities in which they live.

According to the National Standards for Civics and Government (Center for Civic Education 1997, 141–145) the following are the organizing questions around which civic education should be based:

I. What are civic life, politics, and government?

II. What are the foundations of the American political system?

III. How does the government established by the constitution embody the purposes, values, and principles of American democracy?

IV. What is the relationship of the United States to other nations and to world affairs?

V. What are the roles of citizens in American democracy?s

Teachers need to help students understand and respond to these civic questions so that students can apply their knowledge later in life when responding to daily events as adults in a democracy. Experiences during the K–12 school years lay the foundation for students to be able to evaluate situations and defend positions on public issues as well as influence civic life through working and managing conflict (Constitutional Rights Foundation 2000).

In 1998 and 2006, the National Assessment of Educational Progress assessed the civics achievement of students in fourth, eighth, and twelfth grades. "About two out of three American students at grades 4, 8, and 12 have at least a basic knowledge of civics," according to the 2006 test (Lutkus and Weiss 2007). The basic level on the test means students have a fundamental understanding of the civic education content for their grade levels. Further, the results from the 2006 test showed an increase in the fourth grade student scores since the test given in 1998. However, there was no significant change in the average scores at the eighth and twelfth grade levels (Lutkus and Weiss 2007).

The results of this assessment support the belief that civic education needs to be taught in different ways than it is currently being taught. Today's students no longer want to passively sit back and be told what to think. Instead, teachers should use simulations, creative thinking activities, primary sources, and other active learning strategies to help students better understand the country in which they live. This resource, *Elections*, uses all of these strategies to make learning more meaningful for students.

The Importance of Civic Education *(cont.)*

InIn 2000, the Center for Information and Research on Civic Learning and Engagement and the Carnegie Corporation of New York drew together a prestigious team of scholars and practitioners to create a report on civic education and young people. The report, titled *The Civic Mission of Schools*, was released in 2003 and advocates six approaches to increase the civic-mindedness of young people.

Elections utilizes four of these six approaches within the framework of the lesson plans available in this book. The approaches utilized in this resource include the following:

- providing classroom instruction in government, history, law, and democracy
- incorporating discussion of current, local, national, and international issues and events in the classroom
- encouraging student participation in school governance
- encouraging student participation in simulations of democratic process and procedures (Carnegie Corporation 2003)

The report states that by utilizing these approaches in the classroom, students gain more than simple enjoyment. Interesting lessons such as those in this book bring about the following benefits and skills:

- increased written and oral communication
- a working knowledge of government and democracy
- interest in current events
- a higher likelihood of consistent voting and voting on issues rather than personality when an adult

- increased ability to clearly articulate their opinions
- tolerance of differing opinions
- knowledge of how to make decisions even when others do not agree
- increased political and civic activeness as an adult
- appreciation of the importance and complexity of government
- increased civic attitude (Carnegie Corporation 2003)

All of these skills contribute to the goal of becoming a well-rounded, contributing, and responsible member of society outside of the classroom. However, these skills take time to develop and need to be integrated into the curriculum beginning in kindergarten and extending through twelfth grade to be ultimately effective (Quigley 2005). Therefore, teachers have a responsibility to students to provide them with the activities necessary to learn these skills. Utilizing the approaches advocated in *The Civic Mission of Schools* allows teachers the avenues through which to provide strong civic education.

The Importance of Civic Education *(cont.)*

In order for teachers to be effective, civic education needs to be recognized as a key aspect of today's curriculum.

Schools are the only institution with the capacity and mandate to reach virtually every young person in the country. Of all the institutions, schools are the most systematically and directly responsible for imparting citizen norms. Research suggests that children start to develop social responsibility and interest in politics before the age of nine. The way students are taught about social issues, ethics, and institutions in elementary school matters a great deal for their civic development (Kirlin 2005).

Civic education can be taught both formally and informally. Intentional formal lessons imbedded in the curriculum can give students a clear understanding of government and politics and the historical context for those ideas. This instruction should avoid teaching rote facts and give as much real-life context as possible. Informal curriculum refers to how teachers, staff, and the school climate can lead by example and illustrate to students how a working civic community operates (Quigley 2005). When adult role models portray and promote responsible civic engagement, students have a greater conceptual understanding of the formal, civic-based curriculum and how it relates to everyday life.

Using Current Events in Civic Education

Making curriculum relevant to the real world is a goal every teacher strives for, and civic education curriculum should be no different. Using current events in the classroom is one way to make real-world connections.

In a survey completed by the National Center for Education Statistics in 1997, students indicated that they were interested in news that pertained primarily to sports and entertainment. However, students who had taken courses in school that used current events outside of the sports and entertainment industries reported an increased interest in national issues.

Besides making curriculum relevant to students, using current events as part of civic education has other benefits as well. As this book illustrates, current events—such as elections—can be used as the basis for classroom discussions, debates, and cooperative learning activities, as well as magazine and newspaper articles about current events, which can serve as models for nonfiction writing. Students can also build vocabulary, language, reading comprehension, critical thinking and listening skills, and problem-solving strategies (Hopkins 1998). These higher-level thinking skills are important across all the content areas. Using current events in the classroom is an excellent curriculum model that allows teachers to successfully integrate the curriculum and make it meaningful to today's students.

Research-based Strategies for Teaching Civics

Using Simulations and Active Learning

When students experience an event, they are better able to remember that event. Simulations allow students to actively take part in concepts being taught. Simulations often reflect situations found in the real world. This book allows students to become part of the election process. By doing this, students will better understand and remember the concepts that are taught.

In an active learning classroom, teachers serve as facilitators of learning rather than the people who spoon-feed students the content. Andi Stix (2001) describes this change in the structure of the classroom in the following way:

Although the teacher maintains full control, the classroom becomes so highly structured that the teacher's position is elevated to the role of manager. Goals, objectives, and student outcomes continue to be firmly set by the teacher. However, the teacher now facilitates the class and helps students obtain those objectives through a process of discovery rather than through passive involvement.

Building Vocabulary

As Robert Marzano and his associates (2001b) note in the book *Classroom Instruction That Works*, students must encounter words multiple times before they can learn them. *Elections* repeats key vocabulary words throughout the lessons. Therefore, students encounter the same words even though new content is being taught. This helps students make multiple connections with the words and understand them through different contexts.

Marzano and his associates also note that seeing words before they appear in a reading passage can help students better learn the words. By completing the vocabulary activities prior to reading the background information, students are provided with the opportunity to learn and understand new words, thus helping with their comprehension of the background information when it is read. The vocabulary activities and the background information pieces give students a context for the words prior to the actual lesson.

Analyzing Primary Sources

Using primary sources gives a unique view of history that other ways of teaching history are unable to do. Primary sources include newspaper articles, diaries, letters, drawings, photographs, maps, government documents, and other items created by people who experienced events in the past firsthand. Primary sources show students the subjective side of history, as many authors that experienced the same event often retell it in completely different ways. These resources also show students how events affected the lives of those who lived them. Primary sources make history real to students. As students view these historical items, they are then able to analyze the events from various points of view and biases.

Research-based Strategies for Teaching Civics (cont.)

Analyzing Primary Sources (cont.)

This book allows students to evaluate a variety of primary sources. Each lesson contains a quotation, photograph, or document from election history. Students are asked questions and given activities to complete that will help them better understand the election process. Through these activities, students can place themselves in the past and analyze the historical process from various points of view.

Using Graphic Organizers

Graphic organizers are useful tools in helping students understand patterns, ideas, relationships, and connections. Nonlinguistic representation, such as graphic organizers, allows students to better recall the information they have learned (Marzano et al. 2001a).

The brain seeks patterns to make information meaningful (Olsen 1995). Graphic organizers assist students with these necessary connections. Graphic organizers also allow students to organize their thoughts as well as remember the information at a glance.

Research suggests that graphic organizers improve students' overall reading abilities. When graphic organizers are used, reading comprehension improves (Sinatra et al. 1984; Brookbank et al. 1999). In fact, the National Reading Panel (2000) included graphic organizers in its list of effective instructional tools to improve reading comprehension. Further, graphic organizers help students summarize information and create outlines for future writing assignments.

Graphic organizers are used throughout this book. Each lesson contains a graphic organizer that will allow students to summarize, judge, and analyze information given. The graphic organizers give the students the opportunity to think about and better understand the election process and how it relates to them.

Using Bloom's Taxonomy

In 1956, educator Benjamin Bloom worked with educational psychologists to classify levels of cognitive thinking. These six levels are *knowledge, comprehension, application, analysis, synthesis,* and *evaluation.* Bloom's Taxonomy has been used in classrooms for more than 50 years as a hierarchy that progresses from less to more complex. The progression allows teachers to identify the levels at which students are thinking. It also provides a framework for introducing a variety of questions and activities to all students.

The *knowledge* level asks students to recall information. The *comprehension* level asks students to understand and explain facts, often in their own words. The *application* level requires students to use prior knowledge to answer questions, transfer knowledge from one situation to another, and apply situations from the past to today or to themselves. The *analysis* level asks students to break down material and understand how parts relate to a whole. When students complete the *synthesis* level, they create new ideas based on the information they have learned or change ideas to make new ones. And, the *evaluation* level requires students to make judgments based on evidence or support ideas based on evidence given.

Research-based Strategies for Teaching Civics *(cont.)*

Using Bloom's Taxonomy *(cont.)*

Each lesson in this book includes a comprehension check in the form of an activity sheet that lists several activities for students to complete. The activities check for students' understanding in a way that will allow students to be challenged in their thinking. By assigning the various activities based on Bloom's Taxonomy, students can show their understanding of each concept in this book.

Extending Learning through Research

Allowing students to research information is an important skill at any level. And, with the Internet and other technology in classrooms today, it is a skill that students use often. This book allows students to research ideas and concepts based on each lesson. Students are asked to find facts about past elections and turn those facts into activities. The research extension ideas help students summarize information in fun and creative ways. These activities help students find main ideas, focus on key details, and break down ideas into their own thoughts, all of which are important reading comprehension skills. The research extension activities allow students to practice their reading and writing skills.

Making Connections

Students make meaning out of what is taught based on prior understanding, learning styles, and their own attitudes and beliefs. It is important when teaching any concept to help students make connections to themselves, to the past, or to the world in which they live. Many of the activities throughout this book provide students with opportunities to relate the ideas being taught to themselves. Students may be asked to become senators, presidents, or campaign managers. Then, as they research primary sources, they find the connections between past elections and elections today. Finally, as students learn about the election process in democracy, they understand the importance of participating in this process. By making connections, students can better understand and remember the concepts being taught.

Differentiating Activities

Classroom diversity exists throughout the country. Therefore, curriculum must also be diverse. This book provides opportunities for higher-level learners to be challenged, while also providing extra help for struggling students. Each lesson contains differentiation ideas. These ideas include activities for English language learners, below-grade-level learners, and above-grade-level learners, so that all students will be able to complete the simulation activities throughout the book.

Correlation to Standards

Shell Education is committed to producing educational materials that are research- and standards-based. In this effort, we have correlated all of our products to the academic standards of all 50 United States, the District of Columbia, the Department of Defense Dependent Schools, and all Canadian provinces. We have also correlated to the Common Core State Standards.

How to Find Standards Correlations

To print a customized correlation report of this product for your state, visit our website at **http://www.shelleducation.com** and follow the on-screen directions. If you require assistance in printing correlation reports, please contact Customer Service at 1-800-858-7339.

Purpose and Intent of Standards

Legislation mandates that all states adopt academic standards that identify the skills students will learn in kindergarten through grade twelve. Many states also have standards for Pre-K. This same legislation sets requirements to ensure the standards are detailed and comprehensive.

Standards are designed to focus instruction and guide adoption of curricula. Standards are statements that describe the criteria necessary for students to meet specific academic goals. They define the knowledge, skills, and content students should acquire at each level. Standards are also used to develop standardized tests to evaluate students' academic progress.

Teachers are required to demonstrate how their lessons meet state standards. State standards are used in development of all of our products, so educators can be assured they meet the academic requirements of each state.

McREL Compendium

We use the Mid-continent Research for Education and Learning (McREL) Compendium to create standards correlations. Each year, McREL analyzes state standards and revises the compendium. By following this procedure, McREL is able to produce a general compilation of national standards. Each lesson in this product is based on one or more McREL standards. The chart on the following page lists each standard taught in this product and the page number(s) for the corresponding lessons.

TESOL Standards

The lessons in this book promote English language development for English language learners. The standards listed on the following pages support the language objectives presented throughout the lessons.

Correlation to Standards (cont.)

McRel Correlation Chart

Page	Lesson Title	McREL Content Standard
133	The Electoral College	Civics 7.3—Students will know and understand the basis of the Electoral College system
17	Political Parties	Civics 20.1—Students will understand the role of political parties
29, 39, 66	National Elections, State and Local Elections, The Primaries	Civics 20.2—Students will know the various kinds of elections
54, 80, 93	Running for President, The National Convention, The Race Is On!	Civics 20.3—Students will understand the ways in which individuals can participate in political parties, campaigns, and elections, including participating and learning the importance of the national conventions
116	The Vote Is In!	Civics 25.3—Students will understand the importance of such political rights as the right to vote
145	Inauguration Day	Civics 28.6—Students will understand why becoming knowledgeable about public affairs, such as Inauguration Day, is a form of political participation

TESOL Correlation Chart

Page	Lesson Title	TESOL Content Standard
54, 133	Running for President, The Electoral College	2.1—Students will use English to interact in the classroom
17, 80, 93, 116	Political Parties, The National Convention, The Race Is On!, The Vote Is In!	2.2—Students will use English to obtain, process, construct, and provide subject matter information in spoken and written form
29, 39, 66, 145	National Elections, State and Local Elections, The Primaries, Inauguration Day	2.3—Students will use appropriate learning strategies to construct and apply academic knowledge

How to Use This Book

Lesson pacing in this book is very flexible. Each lesson is set up to be taught independent of the other lessons so that teachers can pick and choose just the topics they would like to cover. However, the lessons have been grouped into units, beginning with *What Is Politics?* and concluding with *After the Election*. Within each unit are two to three lessons connected to the unit title. If all lessons are completed in order, students will learn about the entire election process while participating in a mock election of their own.

The Lessons

Most lessons span two to three days. Each day's lesson is intended to take about 60 minutes of class time. The lessons involve the following main parts. Day One is an introduction to the content. This includes a short introductory activity, vocabulary, a reading selection with follow-up activity sheet, and primary source document with a follow-up activity sheet. Day Two begins the lesson's activity. Some activities may require more than one class session. If this is the case, the activity continues on Day Three. Additionally, students have an opportunity to demonstrate their understanding with a Comprehension Check at the end of each lesson. Each day's lesson plan includes step-by-step instructions to help you teach the lessons in a timely manner. The timeline on page 13 may help you plan each lesson.

- **Vocabulary activities** help students understand new words before delving into the background information.

- The **Background Information** page(s) include facts and information students need to fully understand each lesson's topic. Following each information sheet is a student activity sheet. This acts as a follow-up to the information presented in the text. It helps students understand the content within the text, and it holds them accountable for their reading.

- The **primary sources** introduce students to the past through pictures, quotes, documents, or maps. The student activity sheet that follows asks questions related to the primary source to check students' understanding of the document. It also establishes a connection to the lesson's topic.

- **Graphic organizers** are used on most of the activity sheets to help students better understand the topic at hand. The lessons include graphic organizers to check for understanding, help students organize their thoughts, or allow students to summarize information.

How to Use This Book *(cont.)*

The Lessons *(cont.)*

Timeline for Teaching the Lessons

Unit	Lessons	Timeline
Unit 1: Introduction to the Process	Lesson 1: Political Parties	Day 1: Introduce the Content
		Day 2: Begin the Activity
		Day 3: Conclude and Assess
	Lesson 2: National Elections	Day 1: Introduce the Content
		Day 2: Conduct and Assess
	Lesson 3: State and Local Elections	Day 1: Introduce the Content
		Day 2: Conduct and Assess
Unit 2: Getting on the Ballot	Lesson 4: Running for President	Day 1: Introduce the Content
		Day 2: Begin the Activity
		Day 3: Conclude and Assess
	Lesson 5: The Primaries	Day 1: Introduce the Content
		Day 2: Begin the Activity
		Day 3: Conclude and Assess
	Lesson 6: The National Convention	Day 1: Introduce the Content
		Day 2: Begin the Activity
		Day 3: Conclude and Assess
Unit 3: The Campaign Trail	Lesson 7: The Race Is On!	Day 1: Introduce the Content
		Day 2: Begin the Activity
		Day 3: Continue the Activity
		Day 4: Conclude and Assess
	Lesson 8: The Vote Is In!	Day 1: Introduce the Content
		Day 2: Begin the Activity
		Day 3: Conclude and Assess
Unit 4: After the Election	Lesson 9: The Electoral College	Day 1: Introduce the Content
		Day 2: Conduct and Assess
	Lesson 10: Inauguration Day	Day 1: Introduce the Content
		Day 2: Begin the Activity
		Day 3: Conclude and Assess

How to Use This Book *(cont.)*

Lesson Extensions

Differentiation Ideas

For each lesson, suggestions are given to help below-level students, above-level students, and English language learners. Extension ideas are also given to challenge more advanced students or those who finish early.

Research Extension Idea

A research extension idea is available in each lesson. These ideas allow students to further research some of the concepts or terms they have learned in the lesson. After researching, students are given activities to complete based on their research.

Connecting Elections

The lessons in this book mainly focus on the presidential elections. However, each lesson also contains a *Connecting Elections* section that will show students how all elections—from the local and state elections to the national elections—are connected in some way. It will also point out major differences among the various elections when applicable.

Student Activity Sheets

Every lesson contains reproducible student activity sheets that will aid in the teaching of the lesson. Some activity sheets involve maps, while others are lists or cards that students will use during the election simulation. Each lesson includes directions for the use of the activity sheets listed.

Comprehension Check

The Bloom's Taxonomy activities will check students' understanding of the lessons. The activities can be used in several different ways. The rubric on the following page can be used to help you grade this particular part of the lesson. Consider the following methods for assigning activities:

- Assign students activities according to their readiness levels.

- Assign a certain number of activities (such as three), but allow students to choose which activities they would like to do. You could leave this open to student choice, or you could require students to choose at least one activity from the higher-level group and leave the other two choices to them. Students may then choose two additional higher-level activities or they may choose to complete one lower-level and one additional higher-level activity or they may choose two lower-level activities.

- Write the activities on cubes and have the students roll them. The activities that the students roll are the ones they complete. Students may have two to three rolls, depending on how many activities you would like to have them complete.

How to Use This Book *(cont.)*

Comprehension Check *(cont.)*

Comprehension Check Evaluation Rubric				
Name _____				
	4 **Outstanding**	**3** **Good**	**2** **Fair**	**1** **Needs Work**
Completeness	All responses thoroughly complete the assignments.	Most responses complete the assignments, but they may not be thorough.	Some responses complete the assignments, but they may lack thoroughness.	Few or no responses complete the assignments, and they are not thorough.
Accuracy	All responses accurately and correctly provide the requested information.	Responses include mostly accurate and correct information.	Responses include somewhat accurate and correct information.	Responses include mostly inaccurate or incorrect information.
Organization	All responses are well organized, neat, and easily readable.	Responses are mostly organized and legible.	Responses are somewhat organized but may be somewhat illegible.	Responses are poorly organized and may be illegible.
Creativity	All responses are creative, interesting, and have a clear voice.	Responses are mostly creative and interesting but may lack a clear voice.	Responses may lack creativity, interest, and clear voice.	Responses lack creativity, interest and voice.
Vocabulary	All responses include adequate, specific vocabulary.	Most responses use adequate, specific vocabulary.	Some responses use specific vocabulary.	Responses use little to no specific vocabulary.
Appropriateness	All responses are appropriate to format.	Most responses are appropriate to format.	Some responses are appropriate to format.	Few or no responses are appropriate to format.
Conventions	Responses include few, if any, errors in grammar, punctuation, and spelling.	Responses include mostly correct grammar, punctuation, and spelling.	Responses include some incorrect grammar, punctuation, and spelling.	Responses include mostly incorrect grammar, punctuation, and spelling.

TOTAL: _____ / 28

Notes

Lesson 1: Political Parties

Standard

- Students will understand the role of political parties (McREL Civics 20.1)

Vocabulary

- advocate
- conservative
- Democratic Party
- liberal
- political party
- Republican Party

Materials

- *Party Time Background Information* (pages 21–22)
- *Party Time Graphic Organizer* (page 23)
- *Outlining Political Parties of the Past* (page 24)
- *Analyzing Political Parties of the Past* (page 25)
- *Political Parties Primary Source Connection* (pages 26–27)
- *Political Parties Comprehension Check* (page 28)
- Research materials about political parties, current politics, and current news
- Poster boards and other art supplies

Introduce the Content

1. Ask students to list important issues that they face every day. Such issues might include having too much homework, trying not to bend to peer pressure, or having to fit their extracurricular activities into their days. Write these issues on the board. Then, ask the class how they might solve these issues. Record their solutions.

2. Select a problem from the list that has two solutions. Ask those students who are advocates of the first solution to stand on one side of the room. Those who are advocates of the second solution should stand on the other side of the room.

3. While students are all still standing, discuss how solving problems and having different ideas relate to political parties by asking the following questions: *How could supporting different solutions cause conflict? What might happen as a result of this conflict? What if an even less popular solution were suggested? How might the opposing sides resolve their issue?*

 # Lesson 1: Political Parties *(cont.)*

✔ Vocabulary Extension Ideas

- Divide the class into groups of three or four students. Have the groups discuss whether political parties are necessary. Then, have each group write one or two paragraphs explaining their thoughts on the issue and convincing others of their opinions. Have them use all the vocabulary terms to write their paragraphs.

- Ask students to create political picture dictionaries for younger children. Their dictionaries should include the vocabulary words, the definitions, and pictures.

4. Give each student a copy of the *Party Time Background Information* (pages 21–22), *Outlining Political Parties of the Past* (page 24) and *Party Time Graphic Organizer* activity sheet (page 23). Have students read and discuss the information with a partner and complete the graphic organizer.

Differentiation Idea

English language learners may need additional help reading the background information. While other students are reading individually, English language learners can work in small groups with you. Work with these students to help them understand and visualize the vocabulary words.

5. Distribute copies of the *Political Parties Primary Source Connection* activity sheet (pages 26–27) to students. Discuss the picture and information as a class. Allow students to answer the questions in small groups. As an extension, ask them to do the primary source activity.

 ## 2 Day Begin the Activity

1. Begin with a review of political parties. Discuss the difference between Republicans and Democrats. Have students use their activity sheets to guide them.

2. Tell students that they are going to be divided into political parties. Discuss with students whether there should be two or three parties.

3. Once your students decide how many parties to have, divide the class into that number of political parties. You may decide how to divide them, or you may allow students to divide themselves based on how they would solve the issues discussed on Day One.

4. Ask students to create their own political party names. They should also create a symbol to represent the party. Allow them time to create posters that display these names and symbols.

Lesson 1: Political Parties *(cont.)*

5. As homework, have students discuss with their families the issues that today's president faces. Have students bring their lists with them to class tomorrow.

Differentiation Ideas

English language learners may benefit from having specially chosen partners. Place them with students who are strong in English skills, as well as those who have good historical understanding. English language learners can then benefit from the other students' knowledge as they complete their primary source sheets and the other activities throughout the lesson.

Conclude and Assess

Day 3

1. Have students share their lists of issues that affect the president today. You may choose to bring in newspapers or national news magazines to share headlines and determine the issues to supplement students' lists.

2. Discuss with students what a political platform is. Have students determine what the platform is for each party, Democrats and Republicans. Discuss how the beliefs of a party are shared with American citizens.

3. Have students work in their new political parties to create platforms. Their first step is to brainstorm which four or five issues from the class list are most important to them. They need to decide what viewpoint the group has about each issue.

4. Students should then figure out ways to indicate their platforms on their posters.

5. Have each group stand up and present its finished poster to the rest of the class. Summaries should include the party name, symbol, and platform.

6. Distribute the *Political Parties Comprehension Check* activity sheet (page 28) to assess students' understanding of political parties. Use the Comprehension Check Rubric (page 15) to evaluate students' work.

Differentiation Ideas

Work with **English language learners** to ensure that the vocabulary is clear to them. If necessary, look up the vocabulary words with them and discuss the words in context.

 # Lesson 1: Political Parties *(cont.)*

Extension Ideas

☑ Election Quotation Activity

Ask each student to choose one of the following quotations. Then, have students draw their own political cartoons to explain the quotation. They should be sure to write captions for their cartoons.

- "The old parties are husks, with no real soul within either, divided on artificial lines, boss-ridden and privilege-controlled, each a jumble of incongruous elements, and neither daring to speak out wisely and fearlessly on what should be said on the vital issues of the day."

  —*Theodore Roosevelt*

- "There are always too many Democratic congressmen, too many Republican congressmen, and never enough U.S. congressmen."

  —*Author Unknown*

- "How come we choose from just two people to run for president and 50 for Miss America?"

  —*Author Unknown*

> ### Differentiation Idea
> Discuss the quotations with **above-level** students. Encourage them to analyze the quotations and create their own quotations to share with the class.

☑ Research Extension

Have students choose three political parties from American history. They need to research the party platforms as well as find out which presidents (if any) belonged to those parties. Each student can use this information to create a Political Parties Handbook. The list from the *Outlining the Political Parties of the Past* activity sheet (page 24) may be helpful to those students who are struggling with which political parties to research. However, remind them that there are many more political parties than those listed on that page.

☑ Connecting Elections

Strict adherence to the beliefs of one political party can often be a problem on both the national and state levels. When Congress or the state legislatures are dominated by one political party but the president or governors are from another party, the two branches often disagree. Have students give reasons as to why this can be a problem.

Name: _____   Date: _____

Party Time Background Information

Directions: Read the information below.

Political parties first began in 1796. Our country was just forming. Many founding fathers did not want to have such parties, but parties still came into being. People in the parties were concerned with how the new government would be organized.

The first two parties were the Federalists and the Anti-Federalists. The Federalists believed in a strong central government. They believed the United States would be chaotic without a strong government. The Federalists supported the Constitution. They wanted the government to control the building of roads and canals, too.

The Anti-Federalists were later called the Democratic-Republican Party. They had opposing views and supported states' rights. They thought citizens should watch over the people that controlled government. They did not want leaders to get too much power and also thought farmers and craftsmen should help run the government. In other words, they wanted the middle class to take part in running the government, not just the rich.

Party names and ideas have changed over the years. In the 1830s, the Democratic and Whig Parties were formed. Then, in the mid-1800s, the Liberty and Free Soil Parties came into being. The two parties had different ideas about slavery. This caused the parties to split further. The result was the forming of even more political parties.

The two major parties today are the Democratic and Republican parties. The **Democratic Party** is the oldest political party. It began as the Democratic-Republican Party. Thomas Jefferson created it in 1792. Democrats are often thought to take **liberal** positions.

The Democratic Party website states that the party is committed to keeping our nation safe and expanding opportunities for every American. Democrats support strong economic growth. They work toward affordable health care for all Americans. Today, Democrats **advocate** improving the Social Security system. And, they fight for honest government and civil rights.

The **Republican Party** was formed in 1854 by people who opposed the Kansas-Nebraska Bill. They did not want slavery to spread into new states. Abraham Lincoln was a member of this party. He was the first Republican to be elected president. The Republican Party is often referred to as the GOP or Grand Old Party. Today, Republicans are more **conservative** than Democrats.

Party Time Background Information *(cont.)*

The Republican National Committee website describes what Republicans believe. They believe that the strength of our country lies with individuals. Each person's dignity, freedom, ability, and responsibility must be honored. Republicans believe the government needs to be very responsible with money. And, the government should let workers keep more of the money they earn. Government should only provide services that cannot be done by individuals or private groups. Americans should value and preserve our national strength and pride. Finally, Republicans think that Americans should extend peace, freedom, and human rights throughout the world.

Both political parties have symbols to represent them. The donkey has become the symbol of the Democratic Party. This began in 1837. Andrew Jackson was called a donkey by

 his opponents. They said he was stubborn, like a donkey. Jackson decided to use it to his advantage. He began using the picture of a donkey on his campaign posters.

But, Thomas Nast is given credit for creating the donkey symbol. He was a political cartoonist. He used the donkey in an 1874 *Harper's Weekly* cartoon. The Democrats have not officially adopted the donkey as their symbol, but they use it often, such as on campaign advertisements and posters. They see the donkey as humble, homely, smart, and loveable.

 Nast is given credit for creating the Republican Party symbol, too. Their symbol is the elephant. This symbol was also in *Harper's Weekly* in 1874. The Republican Party has adopted this symbol. They view the elephant as having strength and intelligence.

There are only two main political parties that have candidates who run for president. But, third-party candidates may run as well. These parties have ideas that are important to a lot of people. Third parties give citizens more choices when they do not agree with the two main political parties. These third-party candidates often do not win enough votes to win elections. But, they do bring attention to issues. For example, the Prohibition and Socialist parties felt women's rights were important in the 1800s. This led to the Republican and Democratic parties' support of women's rights by the early 1900s.

Name: _____ Date: _____

Party Time Graphic Organizer

Directions: Use the information from the *Party Time Background Information* activity sheet to compare Democrats to Republicans.

Category	Democrats	Republicans
Descriptors	liberal	conservative
Beliefs		
History		
Symbol		

Name: _____ Date: _____

Outlining Political Parties of the Past

Directions: Read the information below.

The following are some of the political parties from the past. They are written in chronological order, from when they first were formed. There are over 50 recognized political parties, though many are very small. Therefore, this is just a small sampling of the political parties throughout America's history.

Federalist Party (1789–1816)—supported a strong central government

Democratic-Republican Party (1792–1824)—opposed a strong central government; later split into multiple parties, including the Whigs; tied to current Democratic Party

Democratic Party (1824–today)—supports liberal policies; one of two main political parties active today

Whig Party (1832–1856)—believed the legislative branch should be more important than the executive branch

Liberty Party (1840–1848)—supported the end of slavery in the United States; joined with others to become the Free Soil Party

Free Soil Party (1848–1855)—believed in "Free Soil, Free Speech, Free Labor, Free Men"; opposed the extension of slavery into the western territories

American Party (1854–1858)—also known as the "Know-Nothings"; opposed immigrants; members often claimed to "know nothing" about the parties' activities

Republican Party (1854–today)—broke away from the Whigs; supports conservative policies; one of two main political parties active today

Greenback Party (1874–1884)—supported paper currency made only by the federal government

Anti-Monopoly Party (1884)—opposed businesses becoming monopolies

Equal Rights Party (1880s)—supported equal rights for women; nominated the first female candidate for president, Victoria Claflin Woodhull

Green Party (1984–today)—supports environmentalism, local control of government, and liberal social policies

Name: _____ Date: _____

Analyzing Political Parties of the Past

Directions: Use the information from *Outlining Political Parties of the Past* activity sheet to answer the questions below.

1. Why does this information page only include a partial list of political parties through time?

_____

_____

2. Which political party lasted the shortest amount of time? Why do you think it did not last very long?

_____

_____

3. Which parties were active during the turn of the twentieth century (around 1900)?

_____

_____

4. Which three parties do you think are the most alike? Explain your answer.

_____

_____

_____

5. If you could join any political party at any time in American history, which would you have joined, and why?

_____

_____

_____

Name: _____ Date: _____

Political Parties Primary Source Connection

Directions: Read the information below.

THE THIRD-TERM PANIC.

Primary Source Background Information

Thomas Nast created this cartoon for the *New York Herald* in 1874. This was in response to the possibility of Ulysses S. Grant running for a third term. Running for a third term was not made unconstitutional until 1951, but it had never been done before. The cartoon was taken from one of Aesop's fables, titled "The Donkey in the Lion's Skin." The moral of the fable is that a fool may disguise his appearance, but his words will reveal who he is. In the cartoon, the *New York Herald* appears as a donkey in a lion's skin. The presence of the donkey frightens the "foolish animals," or other newspapers and magazines.

The fox (at the bottom of the picture) in this cartoon represents the Democratic Party. However, Nast, in later cartoons, depicted the Democratic Party as a tiger and also a donkey. The elephant symbolizes the Republican vote. Both the elephant and fox are near a pit, but the artist does not depict which will tumble into the pit in the upcoming elections. In a later cartoon, after the Republican Party lost in the elections, Nast drew the elephant falling into the pit.

This cartoon is important because it is one of the first times an elephant was used as the Republican Party symbol.

Political Parties Primary Source Connection (cont.)

Primary Source Questions

1. What animals would you select to represent the political parties? Why?

_____

_____

_____

_____

_____

2. Based on this picture and the background information, was it appropriate for the elephant to become the symbol of the Republican Party?

_____

_____

_____

_____

_____

_____

_____

Primary Source Extension

Based on what you have learned about the Republican and Democratic parties, are the symbols they use appropriate? What other symbols might be used instead for each party? Create a new symbol for the Democratic Party and a new symbol for the Republican Party. On a separate sheet of paper, draw your own political cartoon that would show why these new symbols are more appropriate.

Name: _____ Date: _____

Political Parties Comprehension Check

Directions: On a separate sheet of paper, answer the questions below according to the directions from your teacher.

★ Remember

List the two parties that usually hold office today.

★ Understand

Compare the Republican Party to the Democratic Party. Write one paragraph about each party.

★ Apply

Political parties began because many people had different ideas about how the government should be formed. Create a list of other groups that have been formed due to differences in ideas.

★ Analyze

Why is it important for parties to state their platforms? Explain what would happen if parties did not have platforms.

★ Evaluate

Choose five important issues in the news today. List those issues. Then, rate each one on a scale of 1–5, with five being the most important in affecting political parties and their views. Explain why you rated it the way you did.

★ Create

Choose five political parties you have studied. Then, create a symbol for each party that would represent the party's main ideas and platforms.

Lesson 2: National Elections

Standard

- Students will know the various kinds of elections (McREL Civics 20.2)

Vocabulary

- amendment
- candidate
- Constitution
- elected
- election
- representative

Materials

- *National Elections Content-Area Vocabulary* (page 33)
- *Electing Our Leaders Background Information* (page 34)
- *Electing Our Leaders Graphic Organizer* (page 35)
- *The Constitution Rules Primary Source Connection* (pages 36–37)
- *National Elections Comprehension Check* (page 38)
- Three note cards per pair of students
- Research materials concerning electing national leaders

Introduce the Content

1. If you have not completed the previous lessons, review national leaders and political parties with students.

2. Ask students to think about our national government. As a class, create a list on the board of positions that people can hold in our national government. Have students turn to the person next to them and name as many people as they can who hold these government positions.

3. Tell students that many positions in our national government are elected positions, just as the president is elected. However, there are some differences in the election process.

4. Distribute copies of the *National Elections Content-Area Vocabulary* activity sheet (page 33). Have students discuss the terms with a partner and reflect on the class discussion to complete the page collaboratively. You may also ask that they complete a Vocabulary Extension Activity with their partners as well.

✔ Vocabulary Extension Activities

- Ask students to look at the vocabulary words. Then, have them explain ways in which each word applies to a representative, a senator, a president, or another national leader. They can show their explanations on a poster board.

 # Lesson 2: National Elections *(cont.)*

✔ Vocabulary Extention Activities *(cont.)*

- Have each student pretend he or she is a senator or representative. Ask students to create speeches that they may give after being elected.

5. Distribute copies of the *Electing Our Leaders Background Information* activity sheet (page 34). Have students read the information with their partners. Then, have the partners write three important facts from the information, each on its own note card. Collect the cards to use as a review at the beginning of Day Two. Then, have students complete the *Electing Our Leaders Graphic Organizer* activity sheet (page 35) with their partner. Conduct a class discussion using the following questions:

   - Name two ways in which the three positions are alike.

   - Name two ways in which the three positions are different.

   - Which position has the strictest qualifications?

   - Why do you think a senator has a longer term in office than the president and representatives?

6. Distribute copies of *The Constitution Rules Primary Source Connection* activity sheet (pages 36–37) to students. As a class, read the articles from the Constitution aloud. Then, ask students to answer the questions that follow. Have them discuss their answers in small groups. As an extension, ask them to do the primary source activity.

Differentiation Ideas

- Place **English language learners** with **higher-level readers** so that they may ask questions and receive immediate feedback when reading the background information.

- If possible, share photos of the current president and the senators and representatives from your state. Have all students use the photos to sort them into groups: president, senator, and representative.

 # Conduct and Assess

Day 2

1. Use students' fact cards to conduct a review of the information from Day One. Place students with their partners. Randomly distribute three fact cards to each pair of students. Have them read and discuss the information on the cards. Then, have them pass their cards to the partners on their right. Have the pairs read and discuss this second set of cards and then pass them one more time. As a class, ask for volunteers to summarize the information students learned the previous day.

Lesson 2: National Elections *(cont.)*

2. Create a class list of questions students have concerning how each position is elected. Such questions may include *How do the offices get funds for their campaigns? What might persuade or dissuade an incumbent (someone who already holds this office) to run for another term?*

3. Divide students into five or six groups. Give each group a question from the list to research and answer. Depending on the number of questions generated, more than one group may have the same question. Allow students time to do the research.

Differentiation Idea

Help **English language learners** as they research their questions. Give them key words to search as they research. Allow them to write using phrases rather than complete sentences when completing their summaries.

4. Once the groups have found the answers to their questions, come back as a whole class. Then, place students in jigsaw groups (where one student from every question group is represented in each new group), and allow students to share their answers.

5. Distribute the *National Elections Comprehension Check* activity sheet (page 38) to assess students' understanding of national elections. Use the Comprehension Check Rubric (page 15) to evaluate students' work. See page 14 for ideas on how to use this activity sheet with your students.

Extension Ideas

✔ Election Fun Fact Activity

Write the fun fact from below on the board. Then, ask students to think about the fact by asking the following questions: *Why might James Madison have felt this way? Should the representatives and senators have the same qualifications?* Ask students to pretend they are either James Madison or a member of the House of Representatives. If they are James Madison, ask them to defend his thoughts, stating why a senator must have stricter qualifications. If they are representatives, ask them to defend why representatives also must have a "great extent of information and stability of character."

- Senator qualifications are stricter than those of representatives. James Madison, the fourth president of the United States, stated that this was so because a senator called for a "greater extent of information and stability of character."

 # Lesson 2: National Elections *(cont.)*

Extension Ideas *(cont.)*

☑ Research Extension Idea

We all know that the Senate and House of Representatives create laws. But, how do their specific jobs differ? How are they the same? Have students research the jobs of the representatives and senators. Have them then create resumes for both a senator and a representative, stating their job qualifications as well as the types of jobs/activities that they have engaged in as members of Congress. You may wish to bring in sample resumes as examples for students to view before creating their own so that they will know the type of information to include.

☑ Connecting Elections

Many of the senators and representatives get elected on the same date as the president. But the presidential election is much more popular and often overshadows that of the senators and representatives. However, one might say that the elections of senators and representatives are just as important as that of the president. Ask students to discuss this idea by stating how the elections of senators and representatives also greatly affect events that occur in the nation.

Differentiation Idea

As an extension, ask **above-level** students to research specific senators or representatives from history. In their research, ask them to find out what these congressional members did, how they helped change the United States, and other important background information. Then, have students write short biographies of their senators or representatives to be shared with the class.

Name: _____ Date: _____

National Elections Content-Area Vocabulary

Directions: Write the vocabulary word or phrase next to its definition. Choose words from the box below.

amendment	candidate	Constitution
elected	election	representative

Vocabulary Word	Definition
1.	someone who runs for political office
2.	laws written to show how the government will be formed
3.	a law or statement added to the Constitution or another document
4.	selected by voters for an office or position
5.	a person who represents other people or a specific party
6.	the way voters select winners for political offices

Directions: Illustrate each term in the spaces below.

amendment	candidates	Constitution
elected	election	representative

Name: _____ Date: _____

Electing Our Leaders Background Information

Directions: Read the information below.

The President

Every four years, presidents are **elected** for four-year terms. Elections are held on the Tuesday after the first Monday in November. But **candidates** must qualify in order to run for president. The **Constitution** says that a nominee must be a natural-born citizen of the United States. All nominees must be at least 35 years old. And, they must have been a resident of the United States for the past 14 years. Also, the president and vice president cannot live in the same state.

The 22nd **Amendment** of the Constitution limits how long a person can serve as president. A president may only be elected two times or serve for a total of 10 years.

The Senators

Senators are elected for six-year terms. But, senators do not all get elected at the same time. Only one-third of the Senate seats are up for election at one time. And, both seats from the same state are not up for election at the same time. Senatorial **elections** are held every two years.

Each state has two senators. This makes a total of 100 senators in the Senate. At first, the state governments chose their senators. But in 1913, the 17th Amendment changed that. It allowed senators to be elected by the people.

Senate elections are held on the first Tuesday after the first Monday in November. The parties choose their candidates in primary elections. These elections are held several months before the general election.

Senators must be at least 30 years old. They have to be citizens of the United States for at least nine years. They also have to live in the state from which they were elected.

The Representatives

Members of the House of Representatives serve two-year terms. But, they may be reelected for an unlimited number of terms. Each state is represented in the House according to its population. Every state has at least one **representative**. The total number of representatives is 435. This is the most seats there can be. This has been true since 1911.

Elections are also held for representatives on the first Tuesday after the first Monday in November. They are held in every even-numbered year. The candidates are chosen several months before Election Day in a special election called a *primary election*.

There are three qualifications for representatives. Representatives must be at least 25 years old. They must have been citizens of the United States for seven years. And they must live in the state they represent at the time of the election.

Name: _____ Date: _____

Electing Our Leaders Graphic Organizer

Directions: Compare and contrast the election process for presidents, senators, and representatives. Think of areas such as their qualifications, how often they get elected, and their terms in office. Use this graphic organizer to compare all three groups.

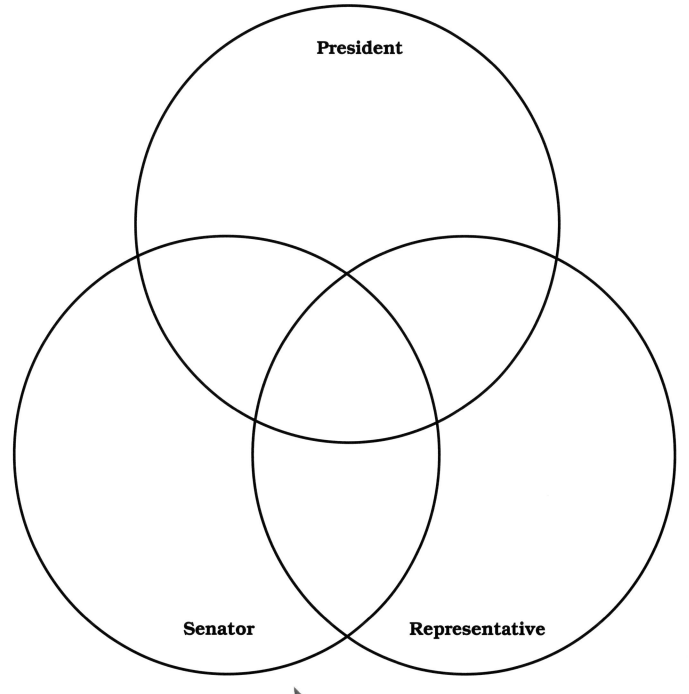

Name: _____ Date: _____

The Constitution Rules
Primary Source Connection

Excerpt from The Constitution of the United States

Article. I.

Section. 1.

All legislative powers herein granted shall be vested in a Congress of the United States, which shall consist of a Senate and House of Representatives.

Section. 2.

The House of Representatives shall be composed of Members chosen every second Year by the People of the several States, and the Electors in each State shall have the Qualifications requisite for Electors of the most numerous Branch of the State Legislature.

No person shall be a Representative who shall not have attained to the Age of twenty five Years, and been seven Years a Citizen of the United States, and who shall not, when elected, be an Inhabitant of that State in which he shall be chosen.

The number of Representatives shall not exceed one for every thirty Thousand, but each state shall have at Least one Representative; and until such enumeration shall be made, the State of New Hampshire shall be entitled to choose three, Massachusetts eight, Rhode Island and Providence Plantations one, Connecticut five, New York six, New Jersey four, Pennsylvania eight, Delaware one, Maryland six, Virginia ten, North Carolina five, South Carolina five and Georgia three.

When vacancies happen in the Representation from any State, the Executive Authority thereof shall issue Writs of Election to fill such Vacancies.

The House of Representatives shall choose their Speaker and other Officers; and shall have the sole Power of Impeachment.

Section. 3.

The Senate of the United States shall be composed of two Senators from each State, for six Years; and each Senator shall have one Vote.

Immediately after they shall be assembled in Consequence of the first Election, they shall be divided as equally as may be into three Classes. The Seats of the Senators of the first Class shall be vacated at the Expiration of the second Year, of the second Class at the Expiration of the fourth Year, and of the third Class at the Expiration of the sixth Year, so that one third may be chosen every second Year.

No Person shall be a Senator who shall not have attained to the Age of thirty Years, and been nine Years a citizen of the United States, and who shall not, when elected, be an Inhabitant of that State for which he shall be chosen.

The Vice President of the United States shall be President of the Senate, but shall have no Vote, unless they be equally divided.

Name: _____ Date: _____

The Constitution Rules
Primary Source Connection *(cont.)*

Primary Source Background Information
The previous page contains excerpts from the Constitution of the United States. The information explains the election process for the legislative branch. The legislative branch is made up of state senators and representatives.

Primary Source Questions

1. How were members of the House and Senate first chosen? How has that changed now?

_____

_____

_____

_____

2. What is the maximum number of representatives, according to the Constitution? What is the number now? Why do you think Congress put an exact number on it?

_____

_____

_____

_____

3. How and why are the senators divided?

_____

_____

4. How can the vice president affect the outcome of a bill in the Senate?

_____

_____

Primary Source Extension
Do you feel the requirements for the senators and representatives are fair? Why or why not? On a separate sheet of paper, defend your answer.

Name: _____   Date: _____

National Elections Comprehension Check

Directions: On a separate sheet of paper, answer the questions below according to the directions from your teacher.

★ Remember

Create a poster that shows the qualifications for senators, representatives, and presidents. Also, include the length of terms in office for each.

★ Understand

Use your vocabulary words. Make a concept map to show the relationship among all six words. A concept map is one picture showing many different parts at the same time.

★ Apply

If you could interview a senator or representative, what questions would you ask? Create a list of 10 interview questions. Then, list how the senator or representative might respond. Use the information you have learned in the lesson for your questions and answers.

★ Analyze

If you had written the Constitution, what qualifications would you have made for senators, representatives, and presidents? Create your own constitution with the new qualifications.

★ Evaluate

Do you think the terms and qualifications for each national elected office are fair? Why or why not? Explain your answer in a letter to Congress, stating whether they should change or keep the current qualifications and justifying your position.

★ Create

Suppose you would like to run for president, but you are an immigrant who has just become a citizen. Therefore, you realize you will never be able to do this. Write a letter to Congress, stating why this qualification is unfair. Then, respond as a congressman/woman, stating why that qualification is necessary and fair.

Lesson 3: State and Local Elections

Standard

- Students will know the various kinds of elections (McREL Civics 20.2)

Vocabulary

- appoint
- government
- governor
- legislation
- vacancy

Materials

- *State and Local Elections Content-Area Vocabulary* (page 43)
- *Our Local Leaders Background Information* (page 44)
- *Electing State and Local Officials* (page 45)
- *State and Local Cards* (pages 46–48)
- *Climbing the Political Ladder* (pages 49–50)
- *Milking the Governor's Cow Primary Source Connection* (pages 51–52)
- *State and Local Elections Comprehension Check* (page 53)
- Internet access for students to research the offices of governor, mayor, and school board in your state, city, and district

Introduce the Content

Day 1

1. If you have not completed the previous lessons, review national leaders and political parties with students.

2. Begin the day by writing the words *state* and *local* on the board. Then, divide students into small groups. Ask them to brainstorm a list of local and state leadership positions in the community as well as state leadership positions. Then, have students turn to the person next to them and name as many people who hold these offices as they can.

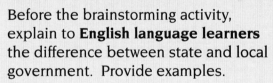

Differentiation Idea

Before the brainstorming activity, explain to **English language learners** the difference between state and local government. Provide examples.

3. Ask students to tell you if each leader is an elected official or a volunteer. Explain that many leaders at the state and local levels are elected officials, just as they are at the national level. This means that they too must go through the same steps as those at the national level in order to get elected.

Lesson 3: State and Local Elections *(cont.)*

4. Distribute copies of the *State and Local Elections Content-Area Vocabulary* activity sheet (page 43) to students. Have students discuss the terms with a partner and reflect on the class discussion to complete the page collaboratively. You may also ask that they complete a Vocabulary Extension Activity with their partners as well.

✔ Vocabulary Extension Activities

- Ask each student to find a news article about a local politician. Have students review their articles, creating summaries that explain what the politicians did. In their summaries, ask students to use at least three vocabulary words.

- Have students find pictures of their mayors and governors. Ask them to write captions below the pictures. Each caption should contain one vocabulary word.

5. Distribute copies of the *Our Local Leaders Background Information* activity sheet (page 44) and the *Electing State and Local Officials* activity sheet (page 45). Read and discuss the information as a class. Then, have students complete the activity sheet.

Differentiation Idea

For **at-risk** and **English language learners**, highlight the information that should be included in the answers about the primary source. Meet with them as a group to review this information.

6. Distribute the *Milking the Governor's Cow Primary Source Connection* activity sheet (pages 51–52) to students. Discuss the photograph and information with the class. Explain to students that governors and other state leaders can often affect national government as well. Ask students how this cartoon shows just that. Then, allow them to answer the questions about the primary source with partners. Finally, discuss the questions.

Conduct and Assess

1. Begin the day by reviewing the graphic organizer that students completed the previous day. Have students share their answers to the questions on page 52 with the class.

2. Cut out the *State and Local Cards* activity sheet (pages 46–48). Divide students into six groups. Give each group one card from each page (three cards total). Have them read their cards and then begin researching the answers to the questions.

Lesson 3: State and Local Elections *(cont.)*

3. Distribute the *Climbing the Political Ladder* activity sheet (pages 49–50) to students. Ask group representatives to state the answers from their cards as the rest of the class records them on their graphic organizers. You may record the answers on the board as well to help those students who need to see the information written.

4. Once the graphic organizers are completed, have students answer the questions on page 50 with their group. As a class, discuss how the information regarding the elections of the governor of your state and mayor of your town compares to the information presented in the *Our Local Leaders Background Information* text (page 44). Summarize the similarities and differences as a class.

Differentiation Idea

As an extension, allow those students who may be interested in political cartoons to find other cartoons that were created about mayors, governors, or other local and state officials. Allow them to analyze the cartoons. You may also ask them to create their own political cartoons concerning state or local officials.

5. Distribute the *State and Local Elections Comprehension Check* activity sheet (page 53) to assess students' understanding of local elections. Use the Comprehension Check Rubric (page 15) to evaluate students' work. See page 14 for ideas on how to use this activity sheet with your students.

Extension Ideas

 Research Extension Idea

Ask students to research the name of the governor of their state or mayor of their town. Then, have them write short biographies about the governor or mayor. You may wish to brainstorm ideas that they might include in their biographies, such as how long the governor or mayor has served, his or her past career in politics, and why he or she got involved in politics. This may be a research project that requires students to contact the office of the governor or mayor.

Connecting Elections

The mayor's title is *His Honor* or *Her Honor*. But, what do we call senators, presidents, governors, and other elected officials? Ask students to research the names of these officials to see how to address them. Then, ask each student to create a list of when and why one may ever need to properly address an elected official.

Lesson 3: State and Local Elections *(cont.)*

Extension Ideas *(cont.)*

☑ Election Quotation Activity

Ask each student to read the quotations listed below. Then, divide the students into small groups. Assign each group a quotation. Have each group create a picture or political cartoon that helps to explain the assigned quotation. Each group should write its assigned quotation at the bottom of its picture. Display the illustrations.

- "The job of mayor and governor is becoming more and more like the job of a university president, which I used to be; it looks like you are in charge, but you are not."

  —*Lamar Alexander, United States senator from Tennessee*

- "As Governor, I could think of only one way to unify our state that was made up of so many different climates, political beliefs and people, and that was our music."

  —*Lamar Alexander, United States senator from Tennessee*

- "I don't want to run for governor, but I don't think anyone should put public service out of the question because that's not what a good citizen does."

  —*Warren Beatty, movie actor*

- "Our recent legislative sessions had everything a good reporter could wish for: A willful governor, an angry and divided legislature, citizens who know how to use their car horns. Plenty of conflict. Plenty of personalities. As journalists, I'm sure it was a fascinating scene to watch unfold."

  —*Phil Bredesen, governor of Tennessee*

- "We remember Ronald Reagan as a man who maximized his gifts from an unknown to an actor to a governor to the leader of the Free World."

  —*Richard Burr, United States senator from North Carolina*

- "Luckily, I'm a governor—so I get to tell you what I've already done, not just what I'm going to do."

  —*Howard Dean, politician from Vermont*

Differentiation Idea

As an extension idea, allow **above-level** students to research governors, mayors, or other local and state officials who went on to run for a national office. Have them create lists of these politicians. They should include where these politicians' political careers began and where their political careers ended.

Name: _____ Date: _____

State and Local Elections Content-Area Vocabulary

Directions: Write the vocabulary word next to its definition. Use all the words from the box.

| appoint | government | governor | legislation | vacancy |

Vocabulary Word	Definition
1.	the system by which a nation or state is run
2.	the act of making laws
3.	the leader of a state
4.	a position that is available for someone to fill
5.	assign or name to a job or duty

Directions: Finish the sentences. Use one word from the word box in each blank.

6. The _____ of the state of Ohio had to _____ someone to run a special project since this person could not be elected.

7. Some people believe in a strong national _____. Other people would rather leave most matters up to the states.

8. The town had to have a special election. One of their local officials left a _____ when she took a job with a private company.

9. The _____ worked very hard with other elected state officials. He wanted to enact a new piece of _____ that he believed would help many citizens.

Name: _____   Date: _____

Our Local Leaders Background Information

Directions: Read the information below.

State House and Senate

Each state has its own House of Representatives and Senate. These bodies meet in each state's capital city to decide on **legislation**. The length of their terms and their qualifications depend upon the state's constitution.

Governor

A **governor** is the leader of a state, as the president is the leader of the country. And, the lieutenant governor is the second in command, just like the vice president.

The qualifications for governor are different from state to state. Most governors serve four-year terms. But in some states, they only serve two-year terms. And in most states, a governor can be elected for an unlimited number of terms. Most governors must be citizens of the United States. They also must meet an age requirement. And most must have been residents of the states in which they were elected for a certain number of years.

In all states, the citizens elect the governor. One role of governor is to veto state bills. The governor can also **appoint** senators if there is a sudden **vacancy** in the United States Senate from his or her state. But the appointed senator only stays in office until the next election. However, not all state **governments** allow their governors to do this.

Mayor

The mayor is the leader of a city. He or she heads the city council, which makes decisions for the city. There are different qualifications for mayor, depending on the state. But citizen voters elect all mayors. Some mayors hold office for two years, but that, too, changes from state to state.

For example, the qualifications in Missouri for mayor are that the candidate must be at least 30 years old. The mayor must be a citizen of the United States. And a mayor in Missouri has to live in that city or town at the time of the elections as well as for one year before.

But, in Montana, a mayor only needs to be 21 years of age. However, they must have lived in the state for three years and in the city for two years.

Other Local Offices

Other local offices can range from city council to the PTA and school board. There are student-body elections, too. Citizens can get involved in many ways, from the local level to the national level.

Name: _____ Date: _____

Electing State and Local Officials

Directions: Use the information from the *Our Local Leaders Background Information* activity sheet to compare the elections between governors and mayors.

Information	Governor	Mayor
What a Leader Does		
Qualifications		
Length of Term		
Who Elects Them		
Other Facts		

1. Why is the office of governor important?

_____

_____

2. Why is the office of mayor important?

_____

_____

State and Local Cards

Teacher Directions: Cut out the cards below and on the following pages.

Governor

What are the qualifications for the governor of your state?	How long is the term for governor in your state?
How many terms may the governor of your state serve?	Who is your governor?
How is your governor elected?	Create your own interesting question concerning the governor's office. Then, answer the question.

State and Local Cards *(cont.)*

Mayor

What are the qualifications for the mayor of your city or town?	How long is the term for mayor in your city or town?
How many terms may your mayor serve?	Who is your mayor?
How is the mayor of your city or town elected?	Create your own interesting question concerning the mayor's office. Then, answer the question.

State and Local Cards *(cont.)*

School-Board Members

What are the qualifications for the school-board members in your district?	How long is the term for school-board members in your district?
How many terms may school-board members in your district serve?	Who is the president or chairperson of your school board?
How are the members of your school board elected? Do they run campaigns?	Create your own interesting question concerning your school board. Then, answer the question.

Name: _____ Date: _____

Climbing the Political Ladder

Directions: Research your own state and local governments. Then, write the qualifications, length of terms in office, how each gets elected, and other important information on the chart below. Finally, answer the questions on the next page.

Government Leader	Qualifications	Length of Terms	How Elected	Other Information
School Board				
Mayor				
Governor				

Climbing the Political Ladder *(cont.)*

Graphic Organizer Questions

1. How are the elections the same for all three offices?

_____

_____

_____

_____

_____

2. Were the qualifications what you expected them to be for each office? Why or why not?

_____

_____

_____

_____

_____

_____

3. Do you think the qualifications are fair for the three offices? Why or why not?

_____

_____

_____

_____

_____

Name: _____ Date: _____

Milking the Governor's Cow Primary Source Connection

Directions: Read the information below.

Primary Source Background Information

This cartoon was drawn in 1861. The cow symbolizes the Union. The man milking the cow is Georgia. The cartoon is referring to South Carolina's governor, Francis Pickens. In early 1861, he attempted to get other Southern states to secede from the Union. In the cartoon, Pickens fights over the cow, hoping to "smash the union." And President James Buchanan vows to prevent it.

Milking the Governor's Cow Primary Source Connection *(cont.)*

Primary Source Questions

1. How does this cartoon show the power a governor can possess?

_____

_____

_____

_____

2. What does the cow, symbolizing the Union, say it will do to the governor? What might this mean?

_____

_____

_____

_____

3. What is written on the cow? Why would having a good Constitution be significant?

_____

_____

_____

_____

_____

_____

Primary Source Extension

Research other powers a governor holds. Then, on a separate sheet of paper, explain how those powers can affect the nation.

Name: _____ Date: _____

State and Local Elections Comprehension Check

Directions: On a separate sheet of paper, answer the questions below according to the directions from your teacher.

★ Remember

List as many elected offices at the local level as you can.

★ Understand

Explain why state and local elections are just as important as national elections. Use information that you have learned throughout the lesson.

★ Apply

You have just won the governor's race. Show how you can affect national government by creating a diagram. Include ideas you have learned throughout the lesson.

★ Analyze

What questions would you ask an elected official at the state or local level? List the questions. Then, tell why you think each question is important.

★ Evaluate

Research and then choose five offices from the state or local levels. Rate these offices in order of importance. Explain your ratings.

★ Create

If you were to run for a local office, which office would you choose? Why? Create a campaign poster for this office. On the poster, include your reasons for running. You may also add a slogan for extra credit.

Lesson 4: Running for President

Standard

- Students will understand the ways in which individuals can participate in political parties, campaigns, and elections (McREL Civics 20.3)

Vocabulary

- campaign
- candidate
- citizen
- delegates
- national convention

Materials

- *Running for President Content-Area Vocabulary* (page 59)
- *In the Running Background Information* (page 60)
- *In the Running Graphic Organizer* (page 61)
- *Running the Race Primary Source Connection* (pages 62–63)
- *Running for Class President* (page 64)
- *Running for President Comprehension Check* (page 65)
- Chart paper and markers
- Online poster-making program (e.g., Glogster™) (*optional*)
- Poster board and art supplies
- Online access to speeches given by recent candidates announcing their candidacies for president, if available

Introduce the Content

1. If you did not do the previous lessons, divide your class into two or three political parties. Have students choose their own parties, or you may assign them to the parties. Allow them to name and create symbols and platforms for their parties.

2. Have students work with partners to list the qualities, traits, or characteristics they believe make a good president. Ask the pairs to brainstorm as many characteristics as they can. Create a class list of characteristics and discuss them as a class. Discuss which single characteristic students believe is the most important. Have each student vote for the one most important characteristic by writing it on a slip of paper. Collect the papers, tally the votes, and circle the top three characteristics. Discuss the results.

3. Discuss the idea of a campaign. Explain that there are many kinds of campaigns, including military, personal, and spiritual. In this unit and the next, students will learn about political campaigns. Distribute the *Running for President Content-Area Vocabulary* activity sheet (page 59). Review the definitions as a class. Then, have students work with a partner to complete the page. You may also ask students to complete a Vocabulary Extension Activity.

Lesson 4: Running for President *(cont.)*

✔ Vocabulary Extension Activities

- Ask students to explain how each word is related to a presidential election. Have them show the relationships on a separate sheet of paper.

- Tell students to pretend they are candidates who are "tossing their hats into the ring." Explain this idiom. Ask students what they might think about becoming president of the United States? Ask students to write down five of their own thoughts concerning what may be going through their minds if they were to become candidates for president. Have them use their vocabulary words.

4. Explain that the process to run for president is more complicated than a person just announcing that he or she will run. Review the qualifications a person must have to run for president (see Lesson 1). Explain that a person must also be supported by his or her party. Distribute the In the Running Background Information activity sheet (page 60) and the In the Running Graphic Organizer activity sheet (page 61) to students. Read and discuss the information as a class. Review the steps that must be in place for a person to run for president. Then allow students to complete the graphic organizer independently or with their group.

Differentiation Idea

List each of the steps to running for president on its own sentence strip. Meet with **struggling students** and **English language learners** in a small group to review the background information. As they read about a step, have one student select that sentence strip and place it at the top of the table. By the end of the reading, students will have ordered each step as it appears in the text. They may use the sentence strips to help them complete the graphic organizer.

5. Distribute the *Running the Race Primary Source Connection* activity sheet (pages 62–63) to students. Discuss the photograph and information with the class. Based on the cartoon, discuss the primary source as a group by explaining the importance of having delegate support. Have students spend a few minutes thinking about how they would answer the questions on the activity page. Then, allow them to share their thoughts and complete this page with partners.

Differentiation Idea

To help **English language learners** and other **struggling students**, read and explain the questions to them.

 **Lesson 4: Running for President** *(cont.)*

 Begin the Activity

Day 2

1. Review the process for becoming a presidential candidate. Students may use their activity sheet from Day One to explain these steps.

2. Discuss whether these characteristics would change if students were thinking about a person running for class president instead of president of the United States. Have students think about important characteristics as they relate to a class president. Add other characteristics to the chart, if needed. Again, poll the students by secret ballot to determine which they believe is the single most important characteristic. Tally the results and circle the top three characteristics.

3. Review the qualifications a person must have to run as a presidential candidate. Then, brainstorm as a class the qualifications the students feel a classroom president should have. Make sure the qualifications are fair so that no student feels left out. Example requirements may be as follows: *must be at least 12 years of age, must be a member of the classroom, and must be a responsible student.* If desired, use an online poster-making program, such as Glogster™ (http://www. glogster.com) to make a class poster titled *Our Classroom Qualifications for President.*

4. Divide students into their political party groups. Allow students to decide whether they wish to run for class president. Explain that two to three candidates can run per party. List these candidates' names on a sheet of paper. Then, have the candidates create support teams to help them with their campaigns. You may choose to divide students into these teams, or you may allow the candidates to choose their own support teams.

5. Allow students and their support teams to create a candidate profile. They may wish to include such information as their likes and dislikes, the party to which they belong, qualifications, campaign promises, and characteristics that would make them a good class president. The *Running for Class President* activity sheet (page 64) may help students organize their ideas. Then, have each support team create a poster detailing their candidate's profile.

6. Allow the candidates to share their profile posters with the class. This way, students can get to know their candidates better.

7. Explain that making speeches is an important part of any campaign. Show the class examples of speeches candidates from the past have given when announcing their candidacies for president. If you are approaching an election year, many speeches can easily be found on the Internet.

 # Lesson 4: Running for President *(cont.)*

8. Discuss with the candidates and support groups what information should be included in their speeches. Then, ask the candidates to create speeches with their support teams. These speeches will announce their candidacies for class president.

9. Allow the candidates to perfect their speeches overnight for homework.

 ## Conclude and Assess

1. Tell students that today is Announcing the Candidates Day. You may wish to hang a banner and have a podium in the classroom for the candidates to use as they announce their candidacies. This will add to the campaign atmosphere.

2. Allow students to give their speeches to the class.

3. Tell students that since they have now "tossed their hats into the ring," they have to begin the next step toward being elected president: gaining delegate support.

4. Review the next step to being elected president from the background informational text. That is, each political party has delegates, or representatives, who promise to support them at the National Convention. (See *The National Convention* lesson, for more in-depth details on the National Convention.)

It is important to gain this delegate support in order to get nominated as your party's candidate.

5. Discuss with students ways in which they can gain delegate support within their parties. Write their ideas on the board. Tell them that they will begin doing these things as they prepare for the primaries in the next lesson.

6. Distribute the *Running for President Comprehension Check* activity sheet (page 65) to assess students' understanding of the presidential election process. Use the Comprehension Check Rubric (page 15) to evaluate students' work. See page 14 for ideas on how to use this activity sheet with your students.

Extension Ideas

 ### ✔ Election Quotation Activity

Write the quotation below on the board. Then, ask the class to break into groups. Ask each group to write a paragraph that would explain what the quotation means. Allow the groups to share their thoughts to see if any of the explanations differed.

- "A politician should have three hats. One for throwing into the ring, one for talking through, and one for pulling rabbits out of if elected."

  —*Carl Sandburg*

 # Lesson 4: Running for President *(cont.)*

Extension Ideas *(cont.)*

✔ Election Quotation Activity *(cont.)*

Then, explain to students that a campaign trail and vying for president requires that candidates wear a lot of hats. Ask students to think about the activities candidates must do when preparing their campaigns by having each student brainstorm a list of other "hats" the politicians must wear. You may choose to bring in articles concerning candidates running for president and the activities they are involved in, such as fund-raising and touring the country. Then, allow students to share their lists. Or, ask them to turn in their lists so that grades can be assigned to them.

✔ Research Extension Idea

Have students research speeches that candidates have given as they enter the presidential race. Then, have students summarize the speeches and critique their content by answering the following questions: *What information about the candidate did this speech include? What information about the issues did the candidate address? Was this an effective speech? Explain why you think this.*

✔ Connecting Elections

All candidates—national, state, and local—must announce their candidacies. Some give speeches. Some announce their candidacies on websites. Ask students, in their opinions, what the best ways are for candidates to "throw their hats into the ring."

Name: _____ Date: _____

Running for President Content-Area Vocabulary

Directions: Look at the words below. Write a definition in your own words for each vocabulary word. Then, write or draw an example for each word.

> **campaign**—an organized effort to achieve a specific goal
>
> **candidate**—someone who runs for political office
>
> **citizen**—a member of a nation or community by birth or other means
>
> **delegates**—people appointed to represent others
>
> **national convention**—an assembly where a candidate is chosen by his or her party to run for president

Vocabulary Word	Definition	Example(s)
campaign		
candidate		
citizen		
delegates		
national convention		

Name: _____ Date: _____

In the Running Background Information

Directions: Read the information below.

Many events happen before an election. First, **candidates** "toss their hats into the ring." This means they announce that they will run in the next election. When this happens, the official **campaign** has begun. Most presidential hopefuls do this by making a speech.

During a nomination campaign, candidates compete from the same party. All candidates running for president hope to get their party's nomination. So, the candidates work to win **delegates** from their parties.

Delegates are representatives from the political parties. These men and women choose who gets to run for president for each political party. Each state gets an assigned number of delegates at the **national convention**. The number of delegates each state gets depends on the number of people living there. The delegates then vote at the convention. The candidate who gets more than 50 percent of the votes becomes that party's nominee. This is the person who will run for president for that party!

But candidates must first qualify to run for president. The Constitution says that a nominee must be a natural-born **citizen** of the United States. All nominees must also be at least 35 years old. And, they must have been a resident of the United States for the past 14 years. Also, the president and vice president cannot live in the same state. The 22nd Amendment of the Constitution limits how long a person can serve as president. One may only be elected two times or serve for a total of 10 years.

These photos of William Taft on the 1908 campaign trail show all the work that goes into running for office.

Name: _____ Date: _____

In the Running Graphic Organizer

Directions: Use the information from In *the Running Background Information* activity sheet to list the steps to becoming a presidential candidate.

1. A person decides to run for president.
2. _____ _____ _____ _____
3. _____ _____ _____ _____
4. _____ _____ _____ _____
5. _____ _____ _____ _____
6. Each party has one presidential candidate.

Name: _____ Date: _____

Running the Race Primary Source Connection

Directions: Read the information below.

Primary Source Background Information

This drawing was created in 1852. It shows Winfield Scott, Daniel Webster, and Franklin Pierce. These men ran for president in 1852. In the cartoon, they are racing for the prize of $100,000. This was the four-year salary for a president.

Webster is leading the race. In the cartoon, he is saying, "I can beat you both, and 'walk in' at that, although you had a hundred yards the start of me." In the primary election, Webster did not get enough delegate votes to win the Whig nomination. So he ran as an independent candidate instead.

Behind Webster is Scott, the man who won the Whig nomination. He is saying, "Confound Webster! What does he want to get right in my way for? If he don't give out, or Pierce don't faint, I shall be beaten."

Pierce trails both of them. He is yelling, "No! No! Old Fuss and Feathers, you don't catch this child fainting now. I'm going in to make good time! Whether I win or not, Legs! Do your duty." (Old Fuss and Feathers was Winfield Scott's nickname.)

It is thought that this cartoon was drawn after Pierce won the Democratic nomination in June. Pierce ended up winning the election as well.

Running the Race Primary Source Connection *(cont.)*

Primary Source Questions

1. What does this cartoon tell us about the 1852 election?

_____

_____

_____

2. When Webster did not win the Whig nomination, what did he do?

_____

_____

3. Pick one person and describe what his actions mean.

_____

_____

_____

_____

_____

_____

_____

_____

Primary Source Extension

The men in this cartoon are racing for a prize: the presidency. But, what are the pros and cons of tossing your hat into the ring? What might they be getting themselves into? Is the prize worth it? Create a pros and cons list on a separate sheet of paper. Base your list on the cartoon, the information from the cartoon, and other background information you have read.

Name: _____ Date: _____

Running for Class President

Directions: You want to run for class president. Think about the qualities or characteristics you have. Think about important issues and where you stand on them. Think about your party and why you want to run. Use this page to plan a poster to illustrate your candidate profile.

Name: _____   Date: _____

Running for President Comprehension Check

Directions: On a separate sheet of paper, answer the questions below according to the directions from your teacher.

★ Remember

List the steps a person must follow to become a presidential candidate.

★ Understand

Draw and label your vision of an ideal candidate. Be creative!

★ Apply

Think about a cartoon character that you believe would make a great class president.
Write a dialogue between you and this cartoon character in which you try to convince
him or her to run for class president. Include the qualities or characteristics you believe
this character possesses that make him or her
a fine candidate.

★ Analyze

Think about the quality or characteristic you believe is the most important
for a presidential candidate to have. Write a campaign slogan for a fictional
candidate that has this trait.

★ Evaluate

What are the good and bad points of the presidential candidate
selection process in the United States? Make a two-column chart
to list both the good and bad points. Include at least two points
in each column.

★ Create

Based on what you know about being a candidate, write a letter to
a fictional candidate, giving advice about throwing his or her hat into the
ring. Describe the qualities or traits that are important to you, and
why these traits are important.

Lesson 5: The Primaries

Standard

- Students will know the various kinds of elections (McREL Civics 20.2)

Vocabulary

- caucus
- closed primary
- open primary
- presidential primary
- primary election
- runoff primary

Materials

- *The Primaries Content-Area Vocabulary* (page 71)
- *The Primary Purpose Background Information* (page 72)
- *The Primary Purpose Graphic Organizer* (pages 73–74)
- *The Primary Vote Primary Source Connection* (pages 75–76)
- *Newsbreak! Simulation Cards* (page 77)
- *Primary Voting Ballots* (page 78)
- *The Primaries Comprehension Check* (page 79)
- News clippings from primary elections, either recently or from the past (*optional*)
- Highlighters

Introduce the Content

Day 1

1. If students did not participate in the previous lessons, discuss political parties with them. Then, divide the class into two or three political parties. Allow students within those parties to declare their candidacies for president.

2. Write the word *primary* on the board. Ask students to brainstorm what they think this word means in relation to politics. List their ideas. Explain that *primary* can mean "first." In politics, this is the first major election in the race to the presidency.

3. Distribute copies of *The Primaries Content-Area Vocabulary* activity sheet (page 71) to students. Read the words and definitions together. Discuss similarities and differences among the types of primaries. Allow students to complete this page with a partner. You may also ask students to complete a Vocabulary Extension Activity.

Lesson 5: The Primaries *(cont.)*

✔ Vocabulary Extension Activities

- Tell students to pretend they are newspaper reporters. What questions might they ask candidates running in the primaries? Have them each write a list of five questions. Each question must use at least one vocabulary word.

- Have students create state primaries scrapbooks. Their scrapbooks should contain 10 important items that one might save from a state primary. Ask the students to create captions for each item in their scrapbooks. Each caption must contain a vocabulary word.

4. Distribute copies of *The Primary Purpose Background Information* (page 72) and the *Primary Purpose Graphic Organizer* activity sheets (pages 73–74) to students. Read and discuss the information as a class. Discuss new information students learned about each type of primary, and allow them to work in small groups to complete their graphic organizers and answer the questions.

Differentiation Idea

Have **struggling** and **English language learners** use highlighters to highlight the name of each type of primary in the text in one color and important related key terms in a second color. Meet with them in a small group and discuss the similarities and differences among the different types of primaries. Encourage students to use their highlighted notes to help them complete the graphic organizer.

5. Distribute *The Primary Vote Primary Source Connection* activity sheet (pages 75–76) to students. Explain that this page shows two primary election results for the Florida House of Representatives. Ask students to read the information in the charts silently and then discuss the information with a partner and answer the questions. Discuss the information as a whole class. As an extension, ask students to do the primary source activity.

Teacher Note: To answer the last question, explain that voter turnout was 25.7 percent on March 23 and 39.1 percent on May 24. Discuss what this means and whether this seems high or low to students.

Begin the Activity

1. Begin by asking students if they know which type of primary is held in your state. Ask for volunteers to review the advantages and disadvantages of each type of primary. Review as a class why the first few primaries are important to the candidates. Then, ask students why later primaries might be of importance as well.

 # Lesson 5: The Primaries *(cont.)*

2. If this is an election year, you may wish to get students more involved in the actual primaries taking place. Do this by dividing students into small groups. Assign each group a candidate who is running for president. Have the groups track how well their candidates do in each state election. They may be able to find this information on the Internet, on the evening news, or in the newspaper. Have them list the state in which the primary was held and the election results. Then, at the end of the primaries, allow students to write conclusions based on their candidates and how the primaries affected their nominations. Ask them to turn in their conclusions the day after the primaries end.

3. Brainstorm with students what events may affect a candidate's popularity. Write their ideas on the board. Such events may include campaign advertising, news events, their families, revelations concerning their beliefs, experiences, allegations, or where they stand on particular issues.

Differentiation Idea

For **English language learners** and **struggling learners**, have actual examples of campaign advertising, news events, revelations, and other events that may affect a candidate's popularity.

4. Have students work in their political parties. Explain to the class that the primary elections are underway for class president. It is very important that the candidates work together with their teams to gain as many delegate votes as possible for the upcoming national convention. However, some major news events have been taking place as well, which may affect the primaries.

5. Cut out and shuffle the *Newsbreak! Simulation Cards* (page 77). Then, allow each team to randomly choose one card. Have the teams read their cards and then create responses to the situations. Their replies may either be for damage control or to further boost their popularity.

6. As the teacher, act as the moderator. Start with one candidate. Read the situation card aloud to the class. Allow the candidate and his or her team to share their reply. Repeat this step for each candidate. Discuss how the situations may have affected the candidates earning delegate support. Discuss the effects of such news items in real politics.

7. Ask students again why later primaries may be of importance. Discuss how events that did not affect earlier primaries may have huge effects on later primaries.

8. Decide as a class which type of primary the class would like to hold: open, closed, or a caucus. Remind students that a caucus is a bit more informal, with speeches given by various supporters of candidates.

 # Lesson 5: The Primaries *(cont.)*

9. Explain that the candidates will have one last chance to persuade their classmates that they should be selected to represent their party at the national convention. Elicit present-day issues that are important to the class, such as lunchroom rules and homework policies, that they want to hear about from the candidates.

10. Allow students to work in groups with their supporters to write their speeches. If a caucus was chosen, allow other supporters to also write speeches. Give students the rest of the class period to write and perfect their speeches.

11. Any speeches that are not completed should be finished as homework.

Differentiation Idea

For an extension, have students bring in news clippings that show how a candidate's popularity has been affected in some way. Ask them to summarize the articles by writing the cause and effect of the news events. If this is not an election year, have students create their own news articles, pretending that a fictional candidate has been affected.

 ## 3 Day Conclude the Activity and Assess Understanding

1. To begin the class period, allow students to deliver their speeches. Remind the class to be polite.

2. Distribute the *Primary Voting Ballots* activity sheet (page 78) to students. You may also wish to have students register to vote prior to this election by having them complete the registration application at the top of this page.

Teacher Tip: Set up voting booths. These can easily be made out of cardboard boxes.

3. Divide the class into "states." Ask each state to vote in the primaries. Then, gather the results from each state. The states do not have to be real states. Instead, as a class, create your own "states," such as the "North Corner" state, that would include students who sit in the north corner of the classroom. Allow students to be creative.

4. Once all students have voted, privately count the votes. It is very important that only you see the votes so that no students get their feelings hurt if they received few or no votes. Once the votes are calculated, tell students that the candidates will be announced at the national conventions. Save the results for *The National Convention* lesson, which begins on page 80. Assigned "delegates" will announce and nominate the winners of their states at the conventions.

 # Lesson 5: The Primaries *(cont.)*

5. As a follow-up, or as a homework assignment, encourage students to continue to follow the candidates in the real primary elections. Ask students to answer the following questions concerning primaries. You may also ask students to answer these questions based on the candidates assigned to them on Day Two.

- Do the candidates' positions change during the course of the campaigns? If so, how?

- Were there reasons for their changes? Do these changes depend on their audience or the responses from the other candidates?

- What effect does the media have on candidates?

- Why might candidates drop out of the race?

6. Distribute *The Primaries Comprehension Check* activity sheet (page 79) to assess students' understanding of national elections. Use the Comprehension Check Rubric (page 15) to evaluate students' work. See page 14 for ideas on how to use this activity sheet with your students.

Extension Ideas

Election Quotation Activity

Ask students to think about the quotation on the following column. Then, ask them why it is just as important to vote in primary elections as it is in the general election. For the primary election, have each student create a poster encouraging people to vote.

- "People often say that, in a democracy, decisions are made by a majority of the people. Of course, that is not true. Decisions are made by a majority of those who make themselves heard and who vote—a very different thing."

—*Walter H. Judd, United States Congressman*

Research Extension

The types of primaries differ from state to state. Have students research the state in which they live. Have them answer the following questions after researching: "What type of primary is held, an open or a closed? Do you agree with this type of primary? Why or why not? Or, is a caucus held in your state? If so, how does it seem to differ from the states that hold primaries? What activities are held at the caucus?" You may also have the students refer to their *The Primary Purpose Graphic Organizer* (pages 73–74) as they answer these questions.

You may choose to hold the same type of primary or caucus in your own classroom as that of the state in which you live, rather than voting as a class as to whether to hold a caucus or primary (see Day Two—Step 8).

Connecting Elections

Primary elections are also held for senators and representatives. However, they do not seem to be as televised. Ask students why this might be so.

Name: _____ Date: _____

The Primaries Content-Area Vocabulary

Directions: Think about each type of primary election. Use the words and definitions below to help you. List the words with their descriptions. Answer the questions.

> **caucus**—a meeting held to decide nominees for political parties
>
> **closed primary**—an election where people can only vote for members of their own party
>
> **open primary**—an election where people can vote for any candidate from any party
>
> **presidential primary**—an election in which nominees are chosen by each party to run for president
>
> **primary election**—an election in which nominees are chosen to represent the different parties in upcoming elections
>
> **runoff primary**—an election after the primary election to decide on the top two candidates

Description	Vocabulary Word
This is an election that happens first.	**1.**
This type of primary is open to anyone.	**2.**
This type of primary is not open to anyone.	**3.**
This type of primary decides who will run for president.	**4.**
This type of primary happens after the first primary.	**5.**
This type of primary is not really an election. It is more like a meeting to decide who will run for election.	**6.**

7. How is a closed primary different from an open primary? _____

_____

8. What might happen during a presidential election if there were no presidential primary?

_____

_____

9. How is a caucus different from an election? _____

_____

10. How are a caucus and an election alike? _____

_____

Name: _____ Date: _____

The Primary Purpose Background Information

Directions: Read the information below.

Primary elections are held when candidates are chosen in different states to represent a political party. Primaries let parties unite and support one candidate.

There are three main types of primaries. **Closed primaries** are held when voters can only vote in the party in which they are members. Voters register for these parties in advance. This means that if a voter is registered as a Democrat, he or she can only vote for the Democratic candidates. He or she may not vote for the Republican candidates. Independents cannot vote in a closed primary. Independents are neither Democrats nor Republicans. A problem with this type of primary is that voters must belong to a party.

In an **open primary**, a voter may vote in any party primary. It does not matter to which party he or she belongs. Many people do not agree with this type of primary. They fear a "raiding" will occur. This is when voters from one party vote in another party's primary. But, they vote for the weaker candidate. By doing this, they hope that it will give their own party's candidates a better chance of winning in the general election. This idea is also called "crossing over." But, open primaries do let candidates focus their campaigns on every voter, not just those from their own parties.

Sometimes, a candidate does not get enough votes to win the primary election. Then, a **runoff primary** is held. A runoff primary is a second primary between leading candidates in the first primary. The top two candidates advance to the general election.

Not all states have their **presidential primaries** on the same day. In the presidential primaries, many eyes are focused on the states that hold the first primaries for the presidential election. Many candidates feel it is important to win in these states. If they do this, then they have a good chance of winning in other states as well. But, many feel that other states should sometimes hold the first primaries as well. They fear that the states that hold their elections last do not have as much input. The states with early primaries get most of the media attention. This gives the voters in those states a lot of power. Candidates who do poorly in the early states often must drop out of the election. But, if lesser known candidates do well in these early primaries, they can often get more media attention and money for their campaigns.

Besides primaries, parties may select their candidates in **caucuses**. A caucus is a meeting of local members of a political party. They meet to nominate candidates for their parties. One example is the Iowa caucuses. It is historically the first state to vote in the primaries. But it holds a caucus, not a primary. During a primary, voters tell which candidate they prefer on a ballot. But a caucus is more like a town hall meeting. People gather in schools and public places. Speeches are given, and people talk about the candidates before voting. Then, an informal vote is taken. After city caucuses, state caucuses are held. Then, there is a state convention. The caucus takes more time and does not attract as many voters. But it does allow voters to find out more about the candidates.

Name: _____ Date: _____

The Primary Purpose Graphic Organizer

Directions: List the pros and cons of an open primary on the left side of the chart below. Do the same for a closed primary on the right side of the chart. Then, answer the questions on the next page.

Open Primaries		Closed Primaries	
Pros	Cons	Pros	Cons

The Primary Purpose Graphic Organizer *(cont.)*

Graphic Organizer Questions

1. Based on your lists, which method seems to be best, an open or closed primary? Why?

_____

_____

_____

2. What is your strongest argument for a closed primary?

_____

_____

3. What is your strongest argument for an open primary?

_____

_____

4. If you were in charge of choosing the type of primary for your state, which one would you choose? Why?

_____

_____

_____

_____

5. Which type of primary do you think most politicians prefer? Explain your answer.

_____

_____

_____

_____

Name: _____ Date: _____

The Primary Vote Primary Source Connection

Directions: Read the information below.

Florida Department of State
Division of Elections
March 23, 2010 Special Primary
House 4
Republican Primary
Official Results
State Representative
District: 4

	Craig Barker	Matt Gaetz	Bill Garvie	Jerry Melvin	Kabe Woods
Total Votes	5,678	6,313	607	728	1,529
% Votes	38.2%	42.5%	4.1%	4.9%	10.3%

Florida Department of State
Division of Elections
March 24, 2011 Special Primary
House 110
Republican Primary
Official Results
State Representative
District: 110

	Frank Lago	Jose Oliva	Rafael "Ralph" Perez
Total Votes	3,213	3,865	2,121
% Votes	34.9%	42.0%	23.1%

Primary Source Background Information

These charts show two special primary election results in Florida. Both elections were to elect state representatives. Use the information to answer the questions on the following page.

The Primary Vote Primary Source Connection *(cont.)*

Primary Source Questions

1. Who won the special primary election for state representative, District 4, on March 23, 2010? What percent of the vote did this person get?

_____

2. Who won the primary election for state representative, District 110, on May 24, 2011? What percent of the vote did this person get?

_____

3. How much time occurred between these two elections?

_____

4. These elections took place on different days, for different state House seats. How else are these two elections different?

_____

_____

5. These elections were both special primary elections. How else are they similar?

_____

_____

6. Would you say that voter turnout was high or low, or can you not tell? Explain your answer.

_____

_____

Primary Source Extension

If it is a primary election year, watch the voting that takes place throughout the primaries. You may choose to watch a race for House, Senate, governor, or president. Then, create a chart that shows which candidates won the primaries for the two major parties. At the end, write a conclusion based on your chart. If it is not an election year, research the latest election that has taken place and chart those results instead.

Name: _____ Date: _____

Newsbreak! Simulation Cards

Directions: Cut out the cards below. Shuffle the cards and distribute them within your team. After you read your card, create a reply to the situation.

Card One

A rumor is swirling that states that you have been giving students the answer sheets for upcoming science tests. What is your response?

Card Four

People have noticed that you have been helping small children cross the street every day after school. Create a short response to share with your classmates, explaining why you feel this is important. It is sure to boost your popularity.

Card Two

It is said that you are coming out with a new advertisement campaign showing your positive attributes and how you help others. It is sure to boost your popularity. Create a poster of this new campaign to show your class.

Card Five

Your past has come back to haunt you! It is said that in the third grade, you quit the scouting group, stating that you just could not get along with others. How will you respond to this allegation before it negatively affects your campaign?

Card Three

Your family life is hard to hide. It is said that you are never willing to allow your younger siblings to participate in any events with you. Some allegations even state that you are quite selfish when it comes to letting your siblings become involved with your plans. How will you respond?

Card Six

Some speculate that you do not have a strong stand on important school issues. Create a speech that will assure your classmates that you indeed have strong beliefs. State those beliefs in your speech to help boost your popularity.

Primary Voting Ballots

Teacher Directions: Cut out the voter application and ballots. Distribute them to students.

Voter Registration Application

Name _____

Date _____ Date of Birth _____

Address _____

_____

Place of Birth _____

Your Political Party Preference _____

Is all the information on this application correct?   ____ Yes   ____ No

Signature _____

Political Party: _____

Candidate One: ☐ _____

Candidate Two: ☐ _____

Candidate Three: ☐ _____

Candidate Four: ☐ _____

Political Party: _____

Candidate One: ☐ _____

Candidate Two: ☐ _____

Candidate Three: ☐ _____

Candidate Four: ☐ _____

Name: _____ Date: _____

The Primaries Comprehension Check

Directions: On a separate sheet of paper, answer the questions below according to the directions from your teacher.

★ Remember

List four different types of primary elections. Also, list details to explain each one.

★ Understand

Explain which two types of primary elections you think are the most alike and which two are the most different. Justify your responses.

★ Apply

Pretend that you are one of the 50 states. Tell which state you are. Then, explain why you want to be either one of the first or one of the last states to hold your primary election.

★ Analyze

In a complete paragraph, explain why primaries are important.

★ Evaluate

Which is better: open or closed primaries? Defend your answer.

★ Create

Develop a plan that would change the primaries so that all states will feel as if their primaries are equally important in deciding who will become the candidates for president. Show your plan on poster board.

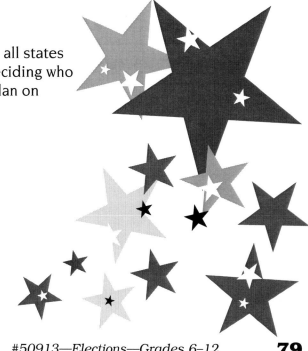

Lesson 6: The National Convention

Standard

- Students will understand the ways in which individuals can participate in political parties, campaigns, and elections, including participating and learning the importance of the national conventions (McREL Civics 20.3)

Vocabulary

- committee
- legitimate
- majority
- party platform

Materials

- *The National Convention Content-Area Vocabulary* (page 85)
- *A Night to Remember Background Information* (page 86)
- *A Night to Remember Graphic Organizer* (page 87)
- *Celebration Night Primary Source Connection* (pages 88–89)
- *Planning the Party* (pages 90–91)
- *The National Convention Comprehension Check* (page 92)
- Footage, videos, or pictures of actual national conventions
- Art supplies (markers, construction paper, glue, scissors)
- Classroom election results from *The Primaries* lesson (see page 69, Day Three, Step 4)

Introduce the Content

Day 1

1. If you did not do the previous lessons, divide your class into two or three political parties at this time. Also, allow students who wish to run for president to make their announcements. If there are a lot of students who wish to run for president from each party, then have a primary election first in which candidates are narrowed down.

2. Tell students that the primaries have ended and that it is now time to officially nominate a candidate. They will be doing this by creating their own parties' national conventions.

3. Write the words *national convention* on the board. Ask students what they think a national convention is. List their ideas.

4. Distribute the *National Convention Content-Area Vocabulary* activity sheet (page 85) to students. Review the definitions as a class. Allow students to work in small groups or with a partner to complete the page. Afterward, have volunteers share their examples and nonexamples for each word with the class. You may also ask students to complete a Vocabulary Extension Activity.

 # Lesson 6: The National Convention *(cont.)*

✔ Vocabulary Extension Activities

- Tell the class that they have been asked by their campaign managers to read poems at their parties' national conventions. Ask each student to write a poem about his or her party's candidate. Their poems should contain all the vocabulary words. Encourage students to share their poems at the national conventions.

- Have students each choose two vocabulary words. Then, ask them to compare and contrast those words on Venn diagrams. Allow students to share their Venn diagrams in small groups so that others may be further exposed to the words that they did not choose.

5. Distribute copies of *A Night to Remember Background Information* (page 86) and *A Night to Remember Graphic Organizer* (page 87) to students. Divide the class into small groups. Have students read the information in their groups and complete the graphic organizer.

Differentiation Idea

Place **English language learners** with students who can help them as they read and answer the questions. These students should have complete understanding of the questions and vocabulary so that they can help explain it to English language learners.

6. Distribute copies of the *Celebration Night Primary Source Connection* activity sheet (pages 88–89) to students. Discuss the pictures. Then, ask them to complete the questions concerning the pictures. Students who do not finish their primary source sheets in class can do so as homework.

✔ Extension Idea

Have students watch actual footage or find pictures of a national convention. They should summarize the events that took place during the convention and explain what they found interesting about the convention as well as what they did not like about the convention. Have them decide if the parties seemed to reach the goals for national conventions. Provide class time for students to share.

 ## Day 2 Begin the Activity

1. Begin this day by reviewing the goals of a national convention.

2. Collect students' primary source sheets, which they should have completed as homework from the previous day. Discuss students' answers to the primary source questions.

3. Explain to students that it is now time to plan their parties' national conventions. Students should already be broken into political party groups. If they are not, divide students into political parties at this time.

 # Lesson 6: The National Convention *(cont.)*

4. Explain to students that one of the major events of the national convention is the nomination of the vice president by the new presidential nominee. Ask students, in their party groups, to think about whom they may want to have as their vice-presidential candidate.

   Point out that many vice presidents are nominated to strengthen the party ticket based on where they are from, their stance on issues, their popularity, or their past experiences. For homework, you may wish to assign students the Research Extension Idea (page 84), which helps them learn more about the history of the vice-presidential nominations.

5. Students must also choose delegates within their party groups. The easiest way to do this is to divide those students who are not nominees into "states" within their parties. Inform the delegates of the winners of their states. Then, the delegates should prepare nominating speeches for the candidate who won that state in the primary. A suggestion for the nomination speech may begin, "The great state of _____ nominates _____ to represent the _____ party for president of our class." Use the voting results from *The Primaries* lesson when nominating the candidates (page 69, Day Three, Step 4).

6. Explain that four main goals of the convention are to approve the party's platform, endorse the nominee for president, endorse the nominee for vice president, and show the party's strength through unity and excitement. Tell students that they will be planning conventions, keeping these goals in mind.

7. Distribute copies of the *Planning the Party* activity sheet (pages 90–91) to students. Explain to the class that this activity sheet will guide them as they plan their parties' conventions. The national convention will last 30 minutes.

8. Explain to students that they should have fun and be creative as they plan their conventions. This is a time for party unity and celebration. They can create their own events for the convention. However, besides the events they create, they must include the following events in their conventions: a keynote speaker, nominating speeches, creation of posters, nominations of both the president and vice president, and a party platform.

9. Students will also need to vote within their parties for the vice-presidential nominee at this time and then announce that nominee at the convention. Or, you may wish to allow each candidate to choose his or her running mate. Then, when a candidate is announced as the party's nominee from the primary results, that candidate can announce his or her choice for a running mate at the convention.

Lesson 6: The National Convention *(cont.)*

Differentiation Idea

Allow **English language learners** and **struggling students** to choose which areas they would like to plan for the conventions.

10. Since the nominees and others will be giving speeches at the convention, you may wish to review items that would be appropriate to include in the speeches. Explain to students that they should have a catchy and creative beginning and ending to their speeches. This will get the audience excited about the candidates. Also, they should include the exciting changes that will take place if their candidates are elected.

11. Give students time in class to complete their graphic organizers. Any speeches that need to be written or other ideas created should be done as homework. You may wish to give students an extra day to complete all of their party plans.

Conclude and Assess

1. Today is the day for the national convention. Allow students to hang their posters and distribute their party gear to the classmates who belong in their parties. Then, encourage students to sit with their parties for their conventions.

2. Ask students to turn in their graphic organizers to you. Divide the class into party groups. Allow up to 30 minutes for the parties to conduct their national conventions simultaneously.

3. Once the conventions have taken place, divide students into small groups within their political parties. Then, write these follow-up questions on the board. Allow students about 10 minutes to answer the questions. Then, come back together as a whole group and discuss their answers.

   - What were two advantages to having a national convention?
   - What were two disadvantages to having a national convention?
   - What parts of the convention did you like best?
   - What parts were most helpful for party strength?
   - How could the convention have been improved?

4. Explain to students that now that candidates have been decided for each party, the campaigns will soon begin!

5. Assess students' understanding of national conventions by having them complete *The National Convention Comprehension Check* activity sheet (page 92). Use the Comprehension Check Rubric (page 15) to evaluate students' work. See page 14 for ideas on how to use this activity sheet with your students.

 # Lesson 6: The National Convention *(cont.)*

Extension Ideas

✔ Election Fun Fact Activity

Write the fun fact from below on the board. Then, ask the class to break into groups. Tell them that the government has decided that an oath should be written for the vice president. Ask each group to create an oath for the vice president. Have the groups share their oaths. For more information on the presidential oath, see page 151 of the *Inauguration Day* lesson.

- Unlike the president, the Constitution does not specify an oath of office for the vice president.

✔ Research Extension

The presidential nominee has not always chosen the vice presidential nominee. Ask students to research how the vice president was chosen in the past. Ask them to include amendments from the Constitution that explain how a vice president will be nominated in their research. Have students create flow charts to show the information they have found in their research. Their flow charts should begin with how the vice president was first nominated and end with how he is now nominated.

✔ Connecting Elections

There are no national conventions for senators or representatives. Ask students if they believe a national convention would be important for the senators and representatives as well. Have them explain their thoughts.

Name: _____ Date: _____

The National Convention Content-Area Vocabulary

Directions: Read the examples and nonexamples for each word. Use the definitions below to help you. Decide which word the examples and nonexamples describe. Write the word in the space. Add one more example and one more nonexample for each word.

> **committee**—a special group that comes together to work on a matter
>
> **legitimate**—lawful or legal
>
> **majority**—the greater number; more than half
>
> **party platform**—the ideas, goals, and principles of a political party

Examples	Vocabulary Word	Nonexamples
financial responsibility tax cuts education _____		Fourth of July stage party _____
Republican Executive Democratic National student council _____		friends family pets _____
genuine real rightful _____		unlawful fake wrong _____
most greater preferred _____		minority lesser minuscule _____

Name: _____ Date: _____

A Night to Remember Background Information

Directions: Read the information below.

The national conventions are a time for parties to announce their nominees for president. This marks the end of the primary elections. Each party has its own convention in the summer of the election year. There are two major conventions. They are the Democratic National Convention and the Republican National Convention. Some third parties hold their own conventions as well.

Each party has a **committee**. These committees design how the national conventions will be run. They start work about a year before the conventions. The committees choose where the conventions will be held. The committee also reviews the list of delegates to make sure they are **legitimate**.

The party is now ready to begin! The convention lasts for four days. The first event is to select a chairperson for the convention. It is often the party's leader from the House of Representatives. This chairperson introduces the convention's events.

Then, a keynote speaker creates the atmosphere for the convention. This speaker is often well known. He or she gets the audience excited about the candidates and the evening's events.

Next, a **party platform** is announced. The delegates vote on the platform. Nominating speeches are then held for each candidate. Other speeches are given for the candidates. The convention often has a partylike tone at this point. The audience rallies for their candidates. Banners wave, songs are sung, and slogans are shown.

Finally, the chairman calls the convention to order. It is time for the delegates to vote.

The states are called in alphabetical order. Delegates are present from all 50 states. There are also delegates from Washington, DC, and other places with American voters. The number of delegates used to equal the number of representatives and senators from each state. But this changed in 1916. Republicans started to give bonuses to states who had voted Republican in the last election. This bonus system is still used today. Republicans have over 2,000 delegates and Democrats have over 3,000 delegates at their conventions. The delegates are chosen differently from state to state. Some states choose them in caucuses. Others ask the governors to appoint them. Some are chosen in primary elections. The delegates cast their votes for their states. The presidential candidate is nominated for that party by a **majority** vote.

The final event is the appointment of the vice-presidential candidate. The presidential nominee names his or her running mate. The vice president has an important job. He or she is next in line to become president. This would happen if the president dies or is removed from office. The vice president also is president of the Senate. The vice president must be a natural-born citizen of the United States. He or she must be at least 35 years old. The vice president also must have lived in the United States for 14 years.

During the convention, songs are sung and posters are shown. The party platform is stated. Through these events, the unity of a party is shown. The nominee is ready to begin campaigning for president!

Name: _____ Date: _____

A Night to Remember Graphic Organizer

Directions: Use the information from A *Night to Remember Background Information* activity sheet to write details about the national conventions below.

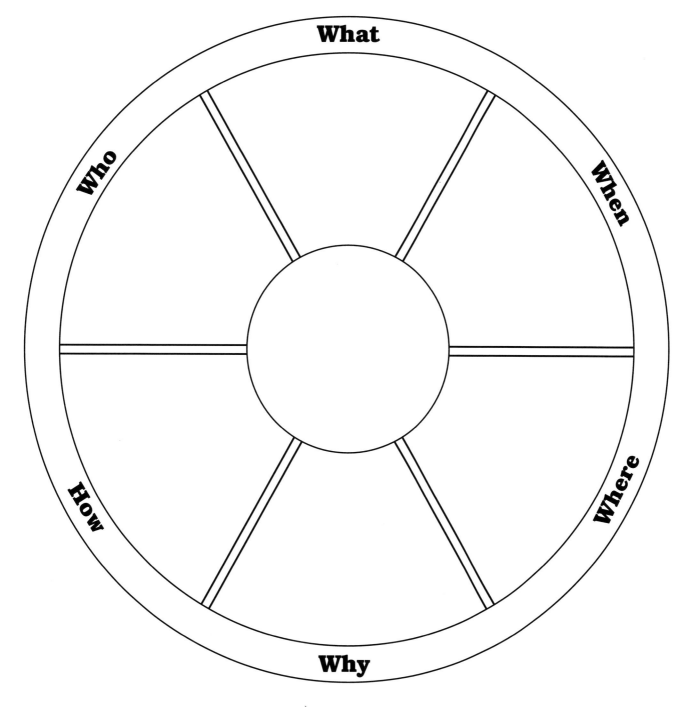

Name: _____ Date: _____

Celebration Night Primary Source Connection

Directions: Read the information below.

Posters of Support	**Celebrating a Nomination**

Primary Source Background Information

These two pictures show the Republican National Convention in Kansas City, Missouri, in August 1976. In the *Posters of Support* picture, state signs are shown to designate the delegates from those states. Delegates supporting Gerald Ford wave posters to show their support.

In the *Celebrating a Nomination* picture, President Ford is nominated as the Republican candidate. He is seen with his wife, First Lady Betty Ford, and his vice-presidential candidate, Robert Dole, and his wife, Elizabeth. They are celebrating their nominations with balloons and speeches.

Celebration Night Primary Source Connection *(cont.)*

Primary Source Questions

1. What type of atmosphere does a national convention appear to have? Give reasons for your answer, based on the pictures.

_____

_____

_____

2. Who is present in these pictures?

_____

_____

3. Most people already know who will be nominated for president based on the results of the primary elections. Based on the pictures and background information, why do you think the national convention is important?

_____

_____

_____

4. In what ways do the parties unite during the national conventions? List two ways the parties unite, using the photographs and background information to support your answer.

_____

_____

_____

_____

Primary Source Extension

People are wearing buttons and hats and carrying posters to show their support. Create your own button or hat to wear or a poster to carry at your party's national convention.

Name: _____ Date: _____

Planning the Party

Directions: Within your group, brainstorm ideas for your party's national convention. What events will be held? In what order will they be held? Write your ideas in the box below. In the chart, list the order in which the events will occur. Finally, list the people who will be in charge of each event in the chart as well as how much time that event should take at the convention.

Planning the Party *(cont.)*

Brainstorming Box

Order of Events	People Responsible	Length
1.		
2.		
3.		
4.		
5.		
6.		
7.		
8.		
9.		
10.		

Name: _____ Date: _____

The National Convention Comprehension Check

Directions: On a separate sheet of paper, answer the questions below according to the directions from your teacher.

★ Remember

Explain what a national convention is. List who organizes it, where it takes place, and when it takes place.

★ Understand

Write a complete paragraph explaining why national conventions are held.

★ Apply

You have just received your formal nomination at the national convention. Create a scrapbook of your night. Include three or more "pictures" with captions. (The pictures can be from the Internet, drawn, or from magazines.) Also include one journal entry describing the event and how it made you feel.

★ Analyze

How would you improve the national convention? List your ideas.

★ Evaluate

Which event in a national convention is the most important? Highlight that event in a news article that explains it.

★ Create

Create a program for a national convention. Include the date, location, and goals of the convention. List events and speakers in the order in which they will take place. Also, acknowledge the committee members that helped put the convention together.

Lesson 7: The Race Is On!

Standard

- Students will understand the ways in which individuals can participate in campaigns (McREL Civics 20.3)

Vocabulary

- campaign
- debate
- endorse
- lobbyist
- media
- propaganda

Materials

- *The Race Is On! Content-Area Vocabulary* (page 101)
- *Hot on the Trail Background Information* (pages 102–103)
- *Hot on the Trail Graphic Organizer* (page 104)
- *Campaigning with Posters Primary Source Connection* (pages 105–106)
- *Joining the Campaign Job Cards* (page 107); 2 copies
- *Account Tracking Task Sheet* (page 108); 2 copies
- *Advertising Staff Cost List of Campaign Materials Task Sheet* (page 109); 2 copies
- *Debate Outline Task Sheet* (pages 110–111); 2 copies
- *Press Secretary Situation Cards Task Sheet* (page 112)
- *Pollster Polls Task Sheet* (page 113); 2 copies
- *Campaign Manager Responsibilities Task Sheet* (page 114); 2 copies

- *The Race Is On! Comprehension Check* (page 115)
- Art supplies
- Paper money (*optional*)
- Examples of campaign advertisements and commercials, if available
- Video of a real presidential debate and candidate speeches (*optional*)
- Audio and video recording equipment
- Current poll results (*optional*)

 ## Introduce the Content

Day 1

1. If you did not do the previous lessons, divide your class into political parties at this time. Allow those students who wish to run for president to announce their candidacies. If there are a lot of students running in each party, have a primary election to narrow down the candidates to one per party. You may also choose to do the national convention activity in *The National Convention* lesson (pages 81–84). Then, continue with step two.

2. Write the following on the board: A *campaign is*…. Ask students to finish this statement. Write their ideas on the board. Explain that a campaign involves propaganda, advertising, speeches, debates, polls, and many other elements. Therefore, it is important that all members of the political parties work together to help their candidates get elected.

 # Lesson 7: The Race Is On! *(cont.)*

3. Distribute *The Race Is On! Content-Area Vocabulary* activity sheet (page 101) to students. Read the definitions as a class. Have students complete this page with a partner. You may also ask students to complete a Vocabulary Extension Activity.

☑ Vocabulary Extension Activities

- Ask students to pretend they are writers for newspapers. Their jobs is to find good quotes to use in articles concerning presidential candidates. Ask students to think about what quotes a candidate running for president might offer. Ask students to then create five quotes that might have come from presidential candidates. They should use a vocabulary word in each of their quotes.

- As students create speeches, posters, and other items for their campaigns, ask them to use at least five to 10 vocabulary words in their campaign projects.

4. Distribute the *Hot on the Trail Background Information* (pages 102–103) and the *Hot on the Trail Graphic Organizer* (page 104) to students. Encourage them to read the information with partners. When they finish reading, have each person ask two or three questions of his or her partner to answer, using information from the text. Then, they can collaborate to complete the graphic organizer.

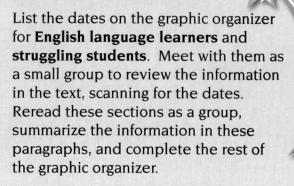

Differentiation Idea

List the dates on the graphic organizer for **English language learners** and **struggling students**. Meet with them as a small group to review the information in the text, scanning for the dates. Reread these sections as a group, summarize the information in these paragraphs, and complete the rest of the graphic organizer.

5. Distribute copies of the *Campaigning with Posters Primary Source Connection* activity sheet (pages 105–106) to students. Discuss the pictures as a class. Then, ask students to complete the questions in small groups within their political parties. Have a class discussion about the campaign posters.

 # Begin the Activity

Day 2

Teacher Note: This part of the election simulation requires different groups of students to be working simultaneously on different tasks. After students have their job assignments, they will split up to work on their respective tasks. As a class organizational strategy, meet with students in joblike groups throughout the process. Check on their progress and answer any questions they may have, as described on the following page.

Lesson 7: The Race Is On! *(cont.)*

1. Have students sit with their political parties. Ask students whom a presidential candidate might depend on throughout his or her campaign. Have them brainstorm with a partner and then share their ideas as a class. Explain that the students will all have a job to do to help get their party's candidate elected.

2. Make two copies and cut apart the *Joining the Campaign Job Cards* activity sheet (page 107). (Make three copies if your class has a three-party campaign.) Randomly distribute one set of cards to six students in each political party. As a class, have a student with a particular job read the information aloud to the class. List the job on the board. Do this for all six jobs.

3. Explain to students that the party will need to collaborate to decide who has which job. In each party, there should be just one student for each job except for the advertising staff. This job may have an unlimited number of students. These six jobs plus the presidential and vice presidential candidates make up the group's political party.

4. Distribute the campaign job task sheets (pages 108–114) to the correct student(s) in each party. Explain that students should read the information on the page and then start working on their part of the campaign.

5. First, meet with the finance managers, advertising staffs, and campaign managers. Explain that the first step to any campaign is securing funds. Explain to students that many lobbyists and special-interest groups give the candidates money. These groups hope that the candidates will support the issues they feel strongly about and change legislation on these issues. Other supporters simply donate money to a candidate because they strongly agree with the candidate and his or her principles.

6. Continue explaining to these joblike groups that they, too, must raise money for their campaigns. They can do this by writing letters to the people described in the list below. They can write any number of letters, but their contributions will be based on how convincing they are (see Teacher Note on the following page). Describe the two types of letters to these joblike groups:

   - Special-Interest Groups: Write a letter explaining how your candidate may help one of these people if he or she gets elected: the librarian, the school nurse, the custodian, the cafeteria staff, or the school secretary. Tell students that they must be realistic in their letters. If they can convince the "special-interest group" of their sincerity, this group may donate money to their cause. Maximum money allowed: $100 per letter.

Lesson 7: The Race Is On! *(cont.)*

- Donations: Write a general letter to the class newspaper asking the public for donations. In your letter, explain why you are working for a candidate that others should support. Your letter will be "published" on the board for others to read. Maximum money allowed: $100.

Teacher Note: Read the letters students write. Use this rating scale to evaluate the students' persuasiveness in each letter submitted: (5)—highly persuasive; (4)—mostly persuasive; (3)—persuasive; (2)—somewhat persuasive; (1)—minimally persuasive; (0)—not persuasive. Then, contribute campaign funds based on the evaluations: $20 per point. So, a letter that has a rating of 4 would earn the candidate $80 for his or her campaign.

7. Once students have received their donations, review the *Account Tracking Task Sheet* (page 108) with the finance manager, campaign manager, and advertising staff. Explain to students that they will need to use their money wisely throughout the campaign to ensure that all advertising techniques can be implemented.

8. Meet with the presidential and vice presidential candidates and the speechwriters. Tell these students that debates are major events in all campaigns. At least two debates are held between the presidential candidates. They are also held between the vice-presidential candidates. Explain that in this campaign, they will engage in one collaborative debate.

9. Explain to students that there are two main types of debates: open forum, in which members of the community ask questions and debates in which moderators ask the questions. Each response is timed and the candidates cannot interrupt each other. They can only defend an answer or respond to the other candidate's statements.

10. Tell students that they will engage in debates in which important issues involving the classroom will be asked. Work with these students to create rules the candidates must follow during the debate. Write them down to review immediately preceding the debate on Day Four. Rules might include talking in a calm voice and not using negative words or gestures (such as eye rolling or heavy sighing). Then, review the *Debate Outline Task Sheet* activity sheet (pages 110–111) with these students. They should work as a team to prepare for the debate.

 Lesson 7: The Race Is On! *(cont.)*

Teacher Note: If desired, write two additional public forum questions on the second page of the *Debate Outline Task Sheet* activity sheet related to current issues among the students in your school.

Differentiation Idea

Have **all students** research or watch presidential and vice-presidential debates. They can use the ideas they glean from their research as part of their own debate strategy.

11. Finally, meet with the Press Secretaries from both parties. Explain that they will need to do some damage control regarding rumors surrounding their candidate by holding a press conference to highlight the positive aspects of their candidate. Review the *Press Secretary Situation Cards Task Sheet* activity sheet (page 112) with these students. Each party should receive one card. Explain that they will need to read over each situation and develop a plan to promote their candidate for both situations.

12. Allow students to continue working on their job tasks for the remainder of the class period. For homework, ask the advertising staff to review both television and radio campaign commercials, if it is an election year.

3 Day — Continue the Activity

1. Distribute the materials from Day Two and encourage students to continue their job tasks from the previous day. Answer any initial questions students may have before they begin working.

2. Meet with the advertising staffs from both parties. Review the work they have accomplished so far. Discuss campaign slogans and why they are important. Tell students that slogans are catchy sayings that tell about the candidate, his or her personality, and often his or her stance on issues. This may be a good time to do the Election Fun Fact Activity and Research Extension Idea found on page 100. One of the advertising staff's tasks is to create a campaign slogan. They will also need to decide how to use it to drum up support for their candidate. The advertising staffs may need to work with the campaign managers if they decide to use more than one slogan.

3. Explain to students that they will also need to brainstorm clever ideas for campaign posters and other propaganda. Allow students time to create their slogans and campaign strategies as a staff. They will need to cash in their money (with the accountant's approval) to purchase the needed supplies.

Lesson 7: The Race Is On! *(cont.)*

4. Dismiss these groups to work on their campaign strategies as an advertising staff. They will need to work closely with the campaign manager to determine the most cost-effective means of advertising their candidate. They should refer to the *Advertising Staff Cost List of Campaign Materials Task Sheet* activity sheet (page 109) to make their advertising decisions.

Differentiation Idea

Encourage **English language learners** to videotape or record their advertisements as if they were on television or the radio.

5. Meet with the pollsters. Explain that the pollster should have been working on creating meaningful polls based on the work of the other campaigners. Review the work they have completed so far based on the *Pollster Polls Task Sheet* activity sheet (page 113). Discuss any questions they have. If possible, show students current poll results from a current poll taken concerning candidates or a current issue involving the president.

6. Guide students to plan how they will conduct the polls and how they will share the results with the campaign manager, the candidates, and the public. Also explain the media they may use to complete their charts (poster paper and markers, or computer printouts, both of which require a fee). Allow the pollsters time to visit other classrooms (if allowed) or adults in the building to conduct their polls. Following this, they should organize the data so that it is easily understood by everyone. They will need to work with the accountants and campaign managers to determine how much they can afford with regard to reporting the results.

Differentiation Idea

As an extension, have **above-level** students to research and find political polls that they can show to the class as examples. Also, ask them to analyze the polls.

7. Encourage students to continue working on their job tasks for the remainder of the class period. Explain that tomorrow is a big day. The candidates will engage in a debate. The advertising staff will air their commercials and display their posters. The press secretaries will make statements related to issues that have arisen during the campaign. The accountants will turn in their financial reports. The pollsters will share their poll results. And the campaign managers will oversee everything!

Lesson 7: The Race Is On! *(cont.)*

Conclude and Assess

4 **Day**

1. Explain that today will conclude the campaign. Hold a brief discussion as a class about the work the students have done to support their candidate.

2. Begin with the advertising staff. Have a spokesperson air commercials and explain their posters and slogans.

3. Have the debate. Encourage the presidential and vice-presidential candidates to stand together. Provide each pair with a podium, if available. Randomly ask questions from the public, one question per student. (Not all students will ask questions.) As the teacher, act as the moderator. Review the rules, and inform the parties of their time limits when speaking (1–2 minutes). Begin the debate with opening statements from each party. Then, ask the moderator questions (page 111). Allow one party to respond first to the first question and the second party to respond first to the second question. Then, open the debate to the public. Call on one student at a time to ask the public-forum questions. Again, alternate parties so that each party has an equal opportunity to respond first. Finally, conclude the debate. Allow each party to give closing statements.

4. Now the press secretaries can present their situations and responses. The class should listen closely. As a class, discuss how these situations both harmed and helped the candidates. Also, evaluate the responses as a class. Discuss whether the press secretaries did a good job with damage control and with positive spotlighting, and why the students think this.

5. Have each pollster share the poll results with the class. Discuss the information and how it might contribute to any future campaign strategies.

6. Have the accountants report their finances to the class. Collect the accountants' financial reports.

7. Distribute the *Campaign Manager Responsibilities Task Sheet* activity sheet (page 114) to students. Discuss the class's experience conducting a campaign. As an evaluation, have each student write a summary explaining his or her role in the campaign, the challenges he or she faced, and the accomplishments he or she is proud of.

8. Distribute *The Race Is On! Comprehension Check* activity sheet (page 115) to assess students' understanding of how people contribute to campaigns. Use the Comprehension Check Rubric (page 15) to evaluate students' work. See page 14 for ideas on how to use this activity sheet with your students.

 # Lesson 7: The Race Is On! *(cont.)*

Extension Ideas

✔ Election Fun Fact Activity

Write the following slogans below from past presidential candidates on the board. Place the students into small groups. Ask them to interpret the slogans, stating the purpose of the slogans and what, if any, promises were made. (The purpose of each slogan is stated below.) Then, as a whole group, discuss their answers. Also ask students to rate the slogans based on how catchy they are as well as their truthfulness. You may even ask students to create other criteria by which to rate the slogans. Vote on the best slogan after the students have rated them.

- "Vote Yourself a Farm"—Abraham Lincoln, 1860 (Refers to the Republican Party's promise of supporting a homestead act that would give free land to those choosing to farm in the West.)

- "A Full Dinner Pail"—William McKinley, 1900 (Refers to the prosperity of the nation under his first administration.)

- "A chicken in every pot and car in every garage"—Herbert Hoover, 1928 (Implies that everyone will prosper under his presidency.)

- "Not Just Peanuts"—Jimmy Carter, 1976 (Jimmy Carter was a peanut farmer. This slogan implies that he has qualifications and experiences other than peanut farming.)

✔ Research Extension

Ask students to research other slogans from past campaigns. Have each student create a collage of these slogans. Then, ask each student to create a slogan that would represent his or her own personality and characteristics. Ask students to add their own slogans to the center of their collages.

✔ Connecting Elections

All candidates, from student body presidents to the United States' president, have campaigns. Have each student compare a local campaign to a national campaign. Ask students how they are similar and how they are different.

Name: _____ Date: _____

The Race Is On! Content-Area Vocabulary

Directions: Use the definitions below to write each word in the correct sentence.

> **campaign**—an organized effort to achieve a specific goal
>
> **debate**—a discussion, usually between two people, in which ideas are given for or against issues
>
> **endorse**—approve of; support
>
> **lobbyist**—a person who tries to persuade politicians to vote for bills they support
>
> **media**—a way to report, write, edit, photograph, or otherwise broadcast news
>
> **propaganda**—information that is spread to promote a person or cause

1. The senator voted against a new law. He did not _____ it.

2. I helped my friend with his _____. We hung posters and gave out cookies at lunch.

3. My mom gets annoyed when a candidate's commercial spreads too much unfair, untrue _____ about his opponent.

4. To get his story heard by all, Ivan went to the _____.

5. The mayor wanted her senator to vote for a new law. So, the mayor went to the state capital and talked with a _____ who talked with the senator.

6. The class was torn. Did we want ice cream or pizza for our class party? Our teacher let us _____ the issue. (The ice cream won!)

Directions: On a separate sheet of paper, draw a campaign scene. Include an example with four or more words from the word box. Label each term.

Name: _____ Date: _____

Hot on the Trail Background Information

Directions: Read the information below.

After the primary elections, candidates begin their campaigns. **Campaigns** are the actions taken by the candidates to get them elected. Candidates hold fund-raisers. They also have **debates**. Commercials, slogans, and speeches are created. And, there is a lot of **media** coverage. Known as **propaganda**, this advertising by the candidates helps them share their views.

In the beginning, candidates did not campaign to win the elections. It was even frowned upon. Candidates waited to be chosen as president. Most were chosen based upon their past work in government. But in 1828, this began to change. Andrew Jackson showed his military experience on buttons and banners. This was used to attract voters. Campaigning was about to begin!

The first campaign slogan was used in 1840 by William Henry Harrison and his running mate, John Tyler. Harrison was a hero at the Battle of Tippecanoe. So, his slogan became, "Tippecanoe and Tyler, too." It was printed on banners and buttons and even used in songs.

Then, with railroads and planes, candidates began to tour the nation. They gave speeches and explained their policies to the people. Today, television and the Internet impact campaigns. Candidates can get their ideas across to more people in less time.

Fund-raising is important to campaigns as well. Many people, known as **lobbyists**, give money to the candidates' campaigns. They do this because they hope the candidates will support their issues when elected. Many lobbyists hope to influence legislation by supporting certain candidates.

Candidates also hold debates during campaigns. The first great debates occurred in 1858. Senator Stephen A. Douglas and Abraham Lincoln held seven debates during their campaigns. They were running for the office of senator in Illinois. The main issue in the debates was slavery. The debates were held outside in seven different cities in Illinois. Crowds came to the events. They would cheer or boo after the statements. The debates were printed in newspapers, too. Lincoln lost the election for senator. But, he got more votes in the counties where the debates were held than he did in the other counties.

In 1960, presidential debates were first shown on television. John F. Kennedy and Richard M. Nixon held four debates. Millions of voters watched the debates or listened to them on radio. Voters noticed the appearance of the two candidates. Kennedy appeared calm and Nixon appeared to be sweating. This caused many to believe he was nervous. Those people who watched the debates felt Kennedy won them. However, those who heard them on radio thought Nixon won them. The candidates' appearance made a difference in the opinions of many people.

Name: _____ Date: _____

Hot on the Trail Background Information *(cont.)*

Media coverage can also affect candidates' campaigns. Candidates try to get more airtime on television or in news publications. They also have photo opportunities. Their pictures are taken with other important people. They hope this will help them gain support. Media can affect the candidates in both negative and positive ways. If a newspaper **endorses** a candidate, it can lead to more support by people who read that newspaper. But, if the media focuses on negative issues or problems, the candidate can lose support as well.

Campaigns are very important to the candidates. During a campaign, candidates get their ideas out to the public. Campaigns include debates, speeches, media coverage, and even bumper stickers. In these ways, candidates show why they should become president of the United States.

Gerald Ford greets supporters at the first presidential debate with Jimmy Carter.

Name: _____ Date: _____

Hot on the Trail Graphic Organizer

Directions: Use information from the text to sequentially organize how campaigns have changed over the past two centuries. List the year of the campaign. List the candidates who participated in the campaigns. List facts about the campaign, especially about how they campaigned (debate, television commercials, and so on). Then, answer the questions below.

Year	Candidates	Campaign Facts

1. How did Jackson's campaign compare to Harrison and Tyler's campaign?

   _____

   _____

2. How did Lincoln's campaign compare to Kennedy's campaign?

   _____

   _____

3. Do you think candidates before radio and television had an advantage or disadvantage when compared to candidates after radio and television? Explain your answer.

   _____

   _____

4. How might the Internet both help and hurt today's candidates?

   _____

   _____

Name: _____ Date: _____

Campaigning with Posters Primary Source Connection

Directions: Read the information below.

Lincoln for President

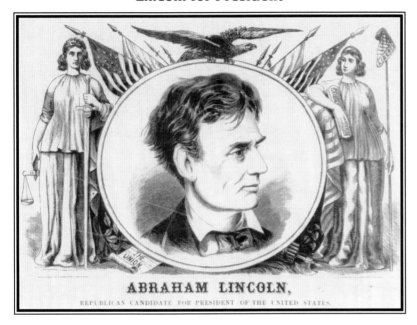

Going Nuts Over Carter

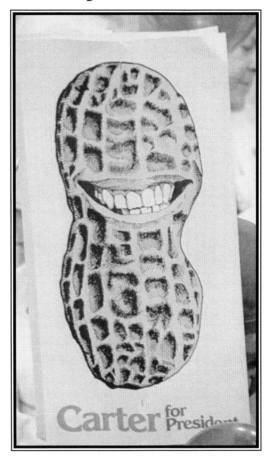

Primary Source Background Information

The *Lincoln for President* campaign poster was created in 1860. It was for the Republican presidential candidate, Abraham Lincoln. The two women standing next to Lincoln's picture represent justice and liberty. Justice holds a scale and a sword. Liberty holds the Constitution and a staff.

The *Going Nuts Over Carter* campaign poster was created in July 1976. It was for the Democratic presidential candidate, Jimmy Carter. It shows a peanut shell with a large smile like Carter's. Jimmy Carter was a peanut farmer prior to running for president.

Campaigning with Posters Primary Source Connection *(cont.)*

Primary Source Questions

1. Name two items that stand out on each poster.

_____

_____

2. How do these two posters, created almost 100 years apart, differ?

_____

_____

3. Do you feel both posters are adequate in showing support for the candidates? Why or why not?

_____

_____

_____

4. List two things that the Lincoln poster tells us about Lincoln and his beliefs. Do the same for the Carter poster. Based on these answers, which poster do you feel tells you more about the candidate?

_____

_____

_____

Primary Source Extension

Pretend you are running for president. What would your campaign poster look like? What symbols might you include on it? Create your own campaign poster on a separate sheet of paper. Be creative and add color!

Name: _____ Date: _____

Joining the Campaign Job Cards

Directions: Cut the cards below apart.

Speechwriter
This person writes speeches with the candidate. Speeches are given to gain support from voters. **You must be very persuasive!** The speechwriter must make sure the speech is powerful, yet professional. Together, the candidate and the speechwriter figure out the details of the speech. Speechwriters must consider the audience and the duration of the speech. The speechwriter should ensure that the ideas are delivered as clearly as possible. The speech should inspire the audience and make them applaud.

Campaign Manager
This person helps the candidate manage his or her campaign. **You must know how to market your candidate so that he or she seems the best!** The campaign manager makes decisions with the candidate that affect the campaign, preferably to help it. This person also helps the candidate stay visible and in a positive light with voters. When things go well, you celebrate with your candidate. But, if things go wrong, you take the blame. Therefore, campaign managers must be confident.

Accountant
This person is the money manager. A successful campaign rests on sufficient funds to run it. Funds come in, and funds get spent. It's your job to keep track of where the money goes and where it comes from. **Therefore, you must be very organized and, most importantly, be good with math!** Additionally, this person reports the campaign finances to the candidate and the public. It is this person's job to be sure the money is spent legally and wisely.

Advertising Staff
This group promotes the candidate. The more people who know about the candidate, the more likely they are to vote for him or her. **You must be very creative!** In an election, the campaign slogan may hold the key. This is one of the jobs of the advertising staff. They must also decide which kind of advertising to use. Of course, the accountant may decline the groups' ideas if they are too costly. So, you must also be able to weigh the cost-benefit when putting together your advertising strategy.

Pollster
Are you nosy? Friendly? Inquisitive? Then you might make a great pollster. This person finds the voters and asks their opinions about the candidates. First, the pollster must develop, plan, and conduct surveys. The results must be communicated to the candidate and the public. Most polls show the results in percentages. So, you must be able to calculate percentages. You must also be able to complete different types of graphs so that everyone can understand the information quickly and easily.

Press Secretary
Press secretaries are public relations specialists. They help the candidate build a relationship with people and the media. They inform people about the activities of the candidate and about his or her accomplishments. **If you are boastful, talkative, and a positive thinker, then press secretary may be the job for you!** This person works closely with the candidate and the advertising staff. Sometimes, the press secretary holds press conferences. Those are speeches about what is happening.

Name: _____ Date: _____

Account Tracking Task Sheet

Directions: Use this tracking sheet to keep track of campaign finances.

Tracking Finances: Write the total amount of donations received for your party in the first box of the *Balance* column. Next, record each purchase in the *Items Purchased* column. Then, write the cost of each purchased item in the *Cost* column. Calculate the balance after each entry. Record it in the last column. See the sample chart below as an example. Be sure the expenses do not exceed the donations! You cannot spend more money than you take in.

Items Purchased	Cost	Balance
		$80.00
3 sheets of paper	$3.00	$77.00
2 audio tapes	$6.00	$71.00

Items Purchased	Cost	Balance

Report the Campaign Finances: On a separate sheet of paper, write a report for the campaign manager. Explain where the donations came from. Explain how the money was spent. Convince the campaign manager that all finances are accounted for and how you kept accurate records.

Name: _____   Date: _____

Advertising Staff Cost List of Campaign Materials Task Sheet

Directions: Use the information on this page to help plan your advertising strategy. You may choose to make posters, flyers, buttons, or commercials to promote your candidate. If you think of other media not listed here, confer with your teacher. Work with the accountant to be sure you can afford all your ideas.

Item	Cost
blank paper	$1.00 per sheet
construction paper	$3.00 per sheet
poster paper	$5.00 per sheet
magic markers	$3.00 per hour or $5.00 for unlimited use
glue	$3.00 per hour or $5.00 for unlimited use
scissors	$3.00 per hour
scotch tape	$1.00 per six inches
masking tape	$2.00 per six inches
use of video camera	$10.00 per hour
air time (via television or radio)	$5.00 per minute
tape recorder	$5.00 per hour
audio tapes	$3.00 each
intercom	$3.00 per minute, if available
wall space	$5.00 per linear foot
door space	$5.00 per linear foot
desk space	$5.00 per desk
ceiling space	$5.00 per string and paper clip
computer use	$10.00 per hour
use of black and white printer	$2.00 per page
use of color printer	$4.00 per page
use of poster printer	$8.00 per sheet

Name: _____ Date: _____

Debate Outline Task Sheet

Directions: Use the information on this page to help you plan for your debate.

Debate Process

This is how the debate will go.

1. Introduction of candidates

2. Opening statements by candidates

3. Moderator questions (see page 111)

4. Public forum (see page 111)

5. Concluding statements by candidates

Things to Think About

1. Will one candidate speak (either the presidential or vice-presidential candidate), or will you share these responsibilities?

2. If only one person speaks, be sure to contrive to plan your debate strategies and responses as a team.

3. If both of you speak, decide who will speak throughout the debate process (see above).

4. After the first question, one party will get to speak first. Then, the second party will have a chance for rebuttal. This is where you agree or disagree with your opponent. Then, after the second question, the second party will get to speak first, and the first party will have a chance for rebuttal. This way, every party has an equal chance to go first.

5. You will only have one or two minutes to respond to the questions or your opponent.

Plan Your Strategy

1. Read the questions that will be asked.

2. State your position.

3. Consider your opponent's position.

4. What will you say if you get to answer first?

5. What will you say if you answer after your opponent?

6. What will you say if you and your opponent agree?

7. What will you say if you and your opponent disagree?

8. Have at least one solid, well-developed explanation or argument to support your position for each question.

9. Plan effective, persuasive statements. You want to appeal to voters even if they disagree with your positions and do not like your ideas.

10. Write your positions and rebuttals on note cards.

11. Practice debating with your team. Be prepared!

Debate Outline Task Sheet *(cont.)*

Moderator Questions

1. Some students like having homework. Other students do not like having homework. What is your position on teachers assigning homework? Do you agree or disagree that homework has value in a student's education? If you agree, what do you believe is an acceptable amount of homework?

2. The school is considering adding lunchroom space, which is much needed. However, this will mean fewer instructional dollars for other events, such as special programs, field trips, and school technology equipment. Where do you stand on this issue, and why?

Public Forum Questions

1. Right now, we only have _____ minutes between classes. This seems unreasonable. We need more time! How might you work with school officials to increase the amount of time students have between classes?

2. I do not feel that students are offered enough choices for lunch. I would like more healthy options and better-tasting options. What is your position regarding the lunchroom selections, and how might you work to improve them?

3. _____

_____

_____

4. _____

_____

_____

Name: _____ Date: _____

Press Secretary Situation Cards Task Sheet

Directions: Read the situations that occur during the campaign. Prepare a statement for each situation to present during a press conference. Your job is to be sure your candidate looks good, no matter what happens!

Party 1 Situations

Situation 1: Your candidate has a younger sister who likes to say mean, untrue things about her older brother or sister. The latest story is that your candidate snuck into the younger sibling's bedroom, drew on her walls with magic marker, and blamed her for the incident, claiming complete innocence. Yikes! Voters will not like a dishonest, sneaky candidate. It appears that they cannot trust this person. Prepare a press statement setting the record straight regarding this allegation.

Situation 2: A story is circulating that your candidate takes in harmed animals and tries to help them heal so that they can be returned to the wild. This story is great news! It makes your candidate seem caring and in touch with the world around him or her. Voters like these qualities in a candidate. But, the story is not true. It is just a rumor. Prepare a press statement regarding this story.

Party 2 Situations

Situation 1: A prank was just played in a neighborhood near school. It left one person's yard a complete mess. The students who did the prank were caught. They claim that your candidate was part of their posse who did the dirty work. Your candidate could be in big trouble! Not only could he or she be punished, but voters will turn away. They want to know a candidate they support is an honest rule follower. But, this allegation is simply not true. Prepare a press statement setting the record straight. You must keep your candidate out of trouble!

Situation 2: A story is circulating that your candidate is a hero! Supposedly, while riding his or her bike in the park, he or she saw a small child who was playing dangerously close to a pond. There were no adults around. Your candidate jumped off the bike and swooped in to pull the child to safety, just before he slipped into the water. He or she spent the rest of the morning trying to find the boy's mother, who was eternally grateful. What a story! Voters like knowing a candidate is willing to drop everything to help the innocent. Unfortunately, this story is not true. It is just fiction. Prepare a press statement regarding this story.

Name: _____ Date: _____

Pollster Polls Task Sheet

Directions: Polling helps candidates stay in touch with the voters. Use this page to help your candidate and the campaign manager run the campaign.

The Campaign Continues

1. The accountant is keeping track of the finances.

2. The president, vice president, and speechwriters are preparing for a debate.

3. The press secretary is working on promoting his or her candidate.

4. The advertising staff is working on "selling" their candidate.

5. The campaign manager is overseeing all aspects of the campaign.

Step 1: Plan
Think about how these people work to run a good campaign. What questions could you ask voters about each part of the campaign? Write one question for each part.

The Debate: _____

_____

The Press: _____

_____

Ads: _____

_____

Overall Campaign: _____

_____

Conduct the Polls

Step 2: Conduct
Choose two questions to ask voters. Prepare a chart to tally their responses. Ask 10 or more people each question. You can ask the same people both questions or poll different people.

Step 3: Chart
Use the data you collected from each poll. Make two charts to show the poll results. The charts should be easy to read and understand. Include a title and label the axes.

Step 4: Report
Report the poll results to the campaign manager and the candidates. You will also report these results to the public.

Name: _____ Date: _____

Campaign Manager Responsibilities Task Sheet

Directions: The success of the campaign rests on your shoulders! Review each person's role in the campaign. Perform each task. Check in with everyone throughout the campaign to be sure things are running smoothly. Help out where you are needed the most.

The Accounts
Your first stop is with the accountant and advertising staff. You must work collaboratively with these team members to secure funds for your campaign. Your teacher has information about how to do this. Once you have secured campaign funds, you must check in with the accountant to be sure the record keeping is accurate.

The Debate
Your candidates will debate several issues. They will work with the speechwriter to plan for and organize their debate strategies. Check in with them to be sure they are persuasive and appealing. Their positions should be truthful but still appeal to voters, even if they disagree with the candidates.

The Press
The press secretary is working on smoothing over a couple of issues that have arisen during the campaign. Check in with this person to be sure the information that will be shared during the press conference holds the candidates in a favorable light.

The Polls
The pollster is working on two polls intended to help guide the campaign. Check in with this person to be sure the questions and responses will help guide the candidates.

Write a sentence or two to explain how you will go about attending to all your responsibilities.

_____

_____

_____

_____

_____

_____

Name: _____ Date: _____

The Race Is On! Comprehension Check

Directions: On a separate sheet of paper, answer the questions below according to the directions from your teacher.

★ Remember

List three events that can help a candidate's campaign. List three events that can hurt a candidate's campaign.

★ Understand

Describe how campaigns have changed over the past 200 years.

★ Apply

A candidate has just asked you, a famous actor/actress, to endorse him or her. What characteristics or ideas would you require a candidate to have in order to endorse him or her? Write those characteristics in a response letter to the candidate. Ask if he or she has these characteristics.

★ Analyze

Research a speech given by a current or past candidate running for office. Then, analyze the speech. Was it factual? Was the truth stretched at times? Write your analysis in paragraph form.

★ Evaluate

What are some challenges people face who participate in campaigns? What do you think is the most rewarding factor regarding people's participation in campaigns? Write a journal entry from the perspective of someone who works on a campaign. Explain how you overcame one challenge and one personal reward or accomplishment of which you are very proud.

★ Create

Create a board game that shows the major steps of a campaign.

 # Lesson 8: The Vote Is In!

Standard

- Students will understand the importance of such political rights as the right to vote (McREL Civics 25.3)

Vocabulary

- ballot
- general election
- polling station
- register
- right
- vote

Materials

- *The Vote Is In! Content-Area Vocabulary* (page 121)
- *Rocking the Vote Background Information* (page 122)
- *Rocking the Vote Graphic Organizer* (page 123)
- *Counting the Vote Primary Source Connection* (pages 124–125)
- *Voter Registration Cards* (page 126); copied and cut apart; one card per student
- *Voter Sign-In Sheet* (page 127); two copies
- *Voting Ballots* (page 128); with candidates' names; cut apart
- *Every Vote Counts* (pages 129–130)
- *Voting Results News Flashes* (page 131); one copy cut apart
- *The Vote Is In! Comprehension Check* (page 132)
- Two shoe boxes
- Wrapping paper or brown grocery bags

 ## Introduce the Content

Day 1

1. If you have not completed the previous lessons, have students divide into two or three political groups. Within those groups, ask them to choose candidates who would like to run for president. Then, follow the voting process in this lesson to allow students to vote for their class president.

2. Write the word *right* on the board. Have students list as many rights as they can think of. Write them on the board all around the word. If students did not mention it, explain that voting is also a right and list it on the board. Discuss why voting is both a right and a responsibility. This may also be a good time to do the Election Fun Fact and Quotations Activity (page 120).

3. Distribute *The Vote Is In! Content-Area Vocabulary* activity sheet (page 121) to students. Review the definitions as a class. Then, allow students to complete this page with a partner. You may also ask students to complete a Vocabulary Extension Activity.

Lesson 8: The Vote Is In! *(cont.)*

✔ Vocabulary Extension Activities

- Have students create "Can You Name the Political Term?" games. Students should create flash cards giving clues for each vocabulary word. They should then write the vocabulary words on the backs of the cards. Encourage students to work with partners to see if they can name the vocabulary words, using the clues.

- Ask students to read newspaper articles or watch the nightly news. Have them then record how many times they hear or see the vocabulary words in the news. Ask them to record the vocabulary words on paper and explain how each word was used in the media.

4. Tell students that they will soon be participating in the general election. Distribute copies of the *Rocking the Vote Background Information* activity sheet (page 122) to students. Have students read the information with a partner. Then, discuss the sheet as a whole class. Read the directions on the *Rocking the Vote Graphic Organizer* activity sheet (page 123) together. Challenge students to review the information from the background information page and complete the sheet.

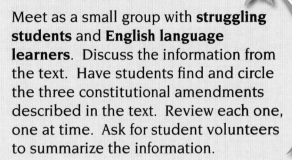

Differentiation Idea

Meet as a small group with **struggling students** and **English language learners**. Discuss the information from the text. Have students find and circle the three constitutional amendments described in the text. Review each one, one at time. Ask for student volunteers to summarize the information.

5. Distribute copies of the *Counting the Vote Primary Source Connection* activity sheet (pages 124–125) to students. Discuss the photograph as a class, listing their observations on the board. Give students time to answer the questions concerning the picture with partners. Then, discuss the answers as a whole class.

6. Explain that tomorrow is voting day! All the students' work on the campaigns will come to a close tomorrow.

Begin the Activity

Teacher Note: Plan ahead. Cover two boxes (shoe boxes will do) with plain wrapping paper or brown grocery bags to act as the ballot boxes. Label one box *North Polling Station* and the second *South Polling Station*. If desired, ask volunteers to further decorate the boxes.

 # Lesson 8: The Vote Is In! *(cont.)*

You may wish to ask parent volunteers to help you with the voting sign-in procedure on Election Day. Set up the polling stations before the students arrive. Each station should have a table where students will sign in to vote. Place one of the ballot boxes at each table.

1. Have students discuss with the person next to them why voting is an important right and responsibility.

2. Remind students that they completed voter registration applications in order to vote in the primary elections (Unit 2, Lesson 5, page 78). Explain that once a person is registered to vote, he or she does not need to do so again. If anyone did not register to vote previously, distribute the *Voter Registration Application* (page 78) for him or her to complete at this time. Copy and distribute the *Voter Registration Cards* (page 126), one per student. Have students complete the information on the card to bring with them to the polling station.

3. Assign the position of "poll worker" to two students, regardless of their political party. One polling station is the "North Corner" and the second station is the "South Corner." Have the two poll workers report to one polling station or the other.

4. Tell students that voting hours will continue through the end of the class period today. They must present their registration cards when voting.

5. Instruct students sitting closest to the North Polling Station to vote there, and those sitting closest to the South Polling Station to vote there. Let students go to their polling stations. Students who made flyers hoping to persuade undecided voters may distribute them as students arrive at the polling stations.

6. The poll workers' job is to be sure every eligible voter displays his or her voter identification and signs in to vote. Use the *Voter Sign-In Sheet* (page 127) for this. Tell students that they must present their voter registration cards before voting. Once they register, they will receive their ballots. (See page 128 for the *Voting Ballots*.) They will vote when the booth is empty. Once students have voted, they should fold their ballots and place them in the appropriate ballot box. You may wish for parent volunteers to help the poll workers sign in the voters and hand out the ballots.

 # Lesson 8: The Vote Is In! *(cont.)*

7. If possible, create "I Voted" stickers ahead of time, using address labels. Or, call ahead to your local Supervisor of Elections office and ask if they have stickers you can hand out to your students. Allow students to wear the stickers after they vote.

8. Once the voting is complete, discuss with students the different ways that changes in technology have affected how people vote. This may be a good time to assign the students the Research Extension Idea (page 120).

9. Assign the *Every Vote Counts* activity sheet (pages 129–130) to students for homework.

Differentiation Idea

As an extension, ask students to watch the real election on television if it is election time. Have them record the results on a blank United States map, showing the election returns as they come in on television.

 # Conclude and Assess

1. Before students come to class, count the votes. Record the results in a way that it appears that the voting was very close at each polling booth to ensure that students' feelings are not hurt. For example: The North Corner polls results:

Candidate One has 49 percent of the votes and Candidate Two has 51 percent. Though this may not be accurate, it will still allow excitement in the classroom when step three below is completed. Record the results on the *Voting Results News Flashes* activity sheet (page 131) and cut the sheet into the three sections.

2. Assign two student volunteers to be news broadcasters. Set up a television station in the room with a table and a backdrop.

3. Discuss as a class the graphic organizers students completed as homework, then collect the pages. During the discussion, have the broadcasters interrupt the class at given times to read the prepared *Voting Results News Flashes* activity sheet. You can even have music to interrupt the class for the special news bulletins.

4. Once the results have been read, explain to students that though it is a time of celebration, the election is still not over. The Electoral College must still place their votes, and in some past elections, the president who won the popular vote did not receive the most votes in the Electoral College. Tell students that the election will continue with the Electoral College in the next lesson.

5. Distribute *The Vote Is In! Comprehension Check* activity sheet (page 132) to assess students' understanding of the voting process. Use the Comprehension Check Rubric (page 15) to evaluate students' work. See page 14 for ideas on how to use this activity sheet with your students.

Lesson 8: The Vote Is In! *(cont.)*

Extension Ideas

✔ Election Fun Fact and Quotations Activity

Discuss the following facts and quotations below with students. Then ask them to create posters that encourage others to vote. On their posters, ask students to use one of the quotes or facts from below, showing how even one vote can make a difference. Students might also choose to create the "Top Ten Reasons to Vote" on their posters, creatively showing why it is important to vote.

- "A citizen of America will cross the ocean to fight for democracy, but won't cross the street to vote in a national election."

  —*Bill Vaughan, author*

- "People often say that, in a democracy, decisions are made by a majority of the people. Of course, that is not true. Decisions are made by a majority of those who make themselves heard and who vote—a very different thing."

  —*Walter H. Judd, author*

- Psephophobia: The fear of voting
- 1645: One vote gave Oliver Cromwell control of England.
- 1649: One vote caused Charles I of England to be executed.
- 1714: One vote placed King George I on the throne in England and restored the monarchy.
- 1800: One vote kept Aaron Burr, later charged with treason, from becoming president.
- 1845: One vote made Texas a state.

- 1850: One vote made California a state.
- 1859: One vote made Oregon a state.
- 1868: One vote saved President Andrew Johnson from being removed from office.
- 1876: One electoral vote gave Rutherford B. Hayes the presidency. The man who cast that one vote was a congressman who was also elected by one vote.
- 1889: One vote made Washington a state.
- 1890: One vote made Idaho a state.
- 1920: Tennessee ratified the 19th Amendment, which allowed women to vote, by one vote. Tennessee was the last state needed for ratification.
- 1923: One vote gave Adolph Hitler leadership of the Nazi Party.

✔ Research Extension

Ask students to research the various ways in which both voting polls and technology in voting have changed. Then, have students create artistic time lines to show these changes by including either drawings or pictures cut from magazines. Use the *Every Vote Counts* graphic organizer to support this extension idea.

✔ Connecting Elections

We vote for the president every four years, but representatives are voted on every even-numbered year, and some senators every two years. Ask the students if they feel these elections are just as important as presidential elections, which often have larger voter participation. Have them state why or why not.

Name: _____ Date: _____

The Vote Is In! Content-Area Vocabulary

Directions: Read the terms and definitions below. Explain in words what each term looks like. Then, draw a picture to illustrate each term.

> **ballot**—a sheet of paper or a card used to cast or register a vote, especially a secret one
>
> **general election**—the final election in which a citizen can vote for the candidates of his or her choice
>
> **polling station**—a place where voters go to cast their votes during an election
>
> **register**—enroll or sign up to vote
>
> **right**—something that is due to a person or governmental body by law, tradition, or nature
>
> **vote**—express one's decision, as in an election

Term	What It Looks Like in Words	What It Looks Like in Pictures
ballot		
general election		
polling station		
register		
right		
vote		

Name: _____ Date: _____

Rocking the Vote Background Information

Directions: Read the information below.

Presidential elections are held every four years. They are held on the first Tuesday after the first Monday in November. This was decided when many people had to make a long journey to the **polling stations**. By early November, crops were in, and the weather was usually not too hot or too cold. So, voters could begin their journeys on Monday and get to the booths by Tuesday to **vote**.

Voting is a **right** for the citizens of the United States. The Constitution states that to vote, you must be 18 years old. You must also be a citizen of the United States. Voting rules are also decided by each state. Some states do not allow felons to vote. Other states do not allow people in jail to vote. Most states allow you to only be **registered** in one state in order to vote.

The Constitution also states certain rights that all voters have. It used to be that only white males owning land could vote. But in 1856, white men without land were given the right to vote. In 1870, voting could no longer be denied on the grounds of race or color. This came about after the Civil War. This right is stated in the 15th Amendment. Also, the 19th Amendment from 1920 tells us that you cannot be denied the right to vote based on whether you are male or female. American Indians were not given the right to vote until 1924. And, the 26th Amendment set the voting age to 18 years. Before that, you had to be 21 years old to vote. The age was changed during the Vietnam War. It was noted that many of the men drafted in the war did not even have the right to vote about the war.

In order to vote, you must register. There are many places you can register to vote. Courthouses, libraries, schools, and other centers make it easy for people to register to vote. Some states even allow voters to register on Election Day at the polls.

Voters cast their **ballots** at polling stations on Election Day. These stations can be schools, libraries, and other public buildings. Each voter is assigned a polling station. Some voters are not able to be present on Election Day. So, they can complete an absentee ballot. This ballot lets voters send in their votes by mail. Some states require a reason for an absentee ballot. Reasons may include travel or sickness. Citizens living outside the United States, such as military personnel, can complete absentee ballots, too. But, a voter must request an absentee ballot before the election occurs.

Citizens cast their votes in the general election with paper ballots or electronic voting machines. On the ballots, each presidential candidate runs together with the vice-presidential candidate. The **general election** is the final election. The votes are counted. One candidate is declared the winner of the political race. However, voters are actually voting for electors in a presidential race. These electors make up the Electoral College. Each state has the same number of electors as it has senators and representatives. In most states, the candidate who receives the most votes gets all of the elector votes. The Electoral College then votes for the president and vice president.

Name: _____ Date: _____

Rocking the Vote Graphic Organizer

Directions: Reread information from the text about how constitutional amendments have changed the right to vote for different groups through history. List details about each amendment in the box below it. Include when the amendment became law, whom the amendment affected, and how the amendment changed the right to vote for these citizens.

```
┌─────────────────────────────────────────┐
│       Constitutional Amendments          │
│       That Changed Voting Rights          │
└─────────────────────────────────────────┘
```

15th Amendment	19th Amendment	26th Amendment

Name: _____ Date: _____

Counting the Vote Primary Source Connection

Directions: Read the information below.

COUNTING THE VOTE, ON NOVEMBER 7TH, AT " ELEPHANT JOHNNIE'S."—FROM A SKETCH BY S. W. BENNETT.

Primary Source Background Information

S. W. Bennett created this sketch in 1876. It shows votes being counted by officials on November 7, 1876—Election Day. It was published in Frank Leslie's illustrated newspaper.

© Shell Education

Counting the Vote Primary Source Connection (cont.)

Primary Source Questions

1. How are the officials keeping track of the votes?

_____

_____

2. Where were the votes placed by the voters?

_____

_____

3. Who do the people standing around appear to be?

_____

_____

4. In what way does this type of voting differ from how votes are counted today? How is the image similar to voting today?

_____

_____

_____

Primary Source Extension

There have been many issues in the news in recent years concerning how to properly count votes so that no errors are made. Pretend you are an inventor. You have been asked by election officials to create a foolproof machine that can guarantee that all votes are counted properly. How might you go about creating such a machine? How would it look? On a separate sheet of paper, draw your design and explain how it works. You may wish to research errors in recent voting to make sure your machine does not repeat the same errors.

Voter Registration Cards

Teacher Directions: Cut the cards below apart.

Voter Registration Card

Name: _____

Address: _____

Signature: _____

Assigned Polling Place: _____

Voter Registration Card

Name: _____

Address: _____

Signature: _____

Assigned Polling Place: _____

Voter Registration Card

Name: _____

Address: _____

Signature: _____

Assigned Polling Place: _____

Voter Registration Card

Name: _____

Address: _____

Signature: _____

Assigned Polling Place: _____

Voter Registration Card

Name: _____

Address: _____

Signature: _____

Assigned Polling Place: _____

Voter Registration Card

Name: _____

Address: _____

Signature: _____

Assigned Polling Place: _____

Name: _____ Date: _____

Voter Sign-In Sheet

Directions: Complete the table below as people vote at the voting center.

Vote Number	Name	Address	Signature
1			
2			
3			
4			
5			
6			
7			
8			
9			
10			
11			
12			
13			
14			
15			
16			
17			
18			
19			
20			
21			
22			
23			
24			
25			
26			
27			
28			
29			
30			

Voting Ballots

Teacher Directions: Cut the cards below apart.

Voting Ballot

Place an X in front of the candidate for whose electors you are voting. Fold the ballot and place it in the ballot box.

_____ Electors for _____

_____ Electors for _____

_____ Electors for _____

Voting Ballot

Place an X in front of the candidate for whose electors you are voting. Fold the ballot and place it in the ballot box.

_____ Electors for _____

_____ Electors for _____

_____ Electors for _____

Voting Ballot

Place an X in front of the candidate for whose electors you are voting. Fold the ballot and place it in the ballot box.

_____ Electors for _____

_____ Electors for _____

_____ Electors for _____

Voting Ballot

Place an X in front of the candidate for whose electors you are voting. Fold the ballot and place it in the ballot box.

_____ Electors for _____

_____ Electors for _____

_____ Electors for _____

Name: _____ Date: _____

Every Vote Counts

Directions: List the pros and cons of counting votes by hand on the chart below. Then, list the pros and cons of having machines count the votes on the computer. Finally, use your lists to answer the questions on the next page.

Pros and Cons of Counting Votes by Hand		Pros and Cons of Counting Votes by Machines	
Pros	Cons	Pros	Cons

Name: _____ Date: _____

Every Vote Counts *(cont.)*

Graphic Organizer Questions

1. What was your strongest argument for counting votes by machine?

_____

_____

_____

_____

_____

2. What was your strongest argument for counting votes by hand?

_____

_____

_____

_____

_____

3. Based on your lists, which type of counting seems to be best? Why?

_____

_____

_____

_____

_____

Name: _____ Date: _____

Voting Results News Flashes

Directions: Cut the cards below apart.

Election Result One

Hello, and welcome to News Channel Five. We are sorry to interrupt your program, but the polls at the North Corner Polling Place have just closed. Officials state that with 30% of the votes in, candidate _____ is leading with 51% of the votes, while _____ is well in to the race with 49%. Stay tuned to News Channel Five for further election results as they come in.

Election Result Two

We now interrupt your program with this special election announcement. The polls in the South Corner have now closed. Forty-five percent of the votes have been counted. And, the race continues to be tight. Candidate _____ has 54% of the votes, while _____ follows closely behind with 46%. With a race this close, the winner can only be determined once all of the votes are counted. We will report the final results as soon as we get them. Stay tuned.

Election Result Three

The votes are in! Candidate _____ has been declared the winner of the popular vote. This is one of the closest races in classroom history. But, with a race this close, we must wait for the Electoral College results to officially declare the next president of the _____ Class.

Name: _____ Date: _____

The Vote Is In! Comprehension Check

Directions: On a separate sheet of paper, answer the questions below according to the directions from your teacher.

★ Remember

Explain the process a person must follow to vote in a general election. List the steps in sequential order.

★ Understand

Describe how three constitutional amendments have changed voting rights for people through United States history.

★ Apply

You have an opportunity to help at the polls during the next general election. Would you accept this offer? Explain why or why not.

★ Analyze

Think about your voting experience. Write a journal entry explaining how you felt when you voted, why you believe your vote made a difference or not, and why you believe the voting process in which you participated was fair and provided accurate results.

★ Evaluate

Some people do not exercise their right to vote. Think about your experience as a voter. List three or more reasons to explain why people may choose not to vote. Then, write counterreasons to convince people that they should vote. For example, if one of your reasons is that it is too hard to get to the polls, counter this argument by explaining how people can vote using an absentee ballot.

★ Create

Create a collage to encourage others to vote. Include facts about voting, such as that it is every eligible citizen's right, and how constitutional amendments have guaranteed this right to all groups of people through history. Be creative.

Lesson 9: The Electoral College

Standard

- Students will know and understand the basis of the Electoral College system (McREL Civics 7.3)

Vocabulary

- elector
- Electoral College
- pledge
- popular vote

Materials

- The Electoral College Content-Area Vocabulary (page 137)
- The Electoral College Background Information (page 138)
- The Electoral College (page 139)
- Mapping the Electoral College Primary Source Connection (pages 140–141)
- The Electoral College vs. the Popular Vote (pages 142–143) (optional)
- The Electoral College Comprehension Check (page 144)

Introduce the Content

1. If you are doing only a lesson on the Electoral College, first review with the class the process for voting in a general election. Then, choose two student volunteers who will pretend to be candidates running for president.

2. Tell students that the votes are in, but the race is close. Explain that the winner of a presidential election is not determined by popular vote. Instead, the winner is declared following the Electoral College system. Therefore, no one will know for sure who has won the presidential election until the Electoral College casts its votes. Have students discuss with a partner what this might mean.

3. Distribute The Electoral College Content-Area Vocabulary activity sheet (page 137) to students. Read the definitions as a class. Read the directions. Complete the first two terms as a class. Then, encourage students to work with a partner to complete the last two terms. You may also ask students to complete a Vocabulary Extension Activity.

 # Lesson 9: The Electoral College *(cont.)*

Vocabulary Extension Activities

- Have students create political cartoons that show whether they agree or disagree with having an Electoral College. They should use at least five vocabulary words somewhere on their cartoons, such as in their titles, in the words of the characters, or in their captions.

- Have students write three or more examples for each of the words. For example, students might list *representatives, outsourcing,* or *hiring* for the *Electoral College.*

4. Distribute T*he Electoral Background Information* (page 138) and T*he Electoral College* (page 139) to students. Allow them to read the information in small groups. After reading, ask the groups to list five important facts concerning the Electoral College. Discuss students' lists as a whole class. Have students complete T*he Electoral College.*

5. Have students guess which state has the most electoral votes and which state(s) have the least. They can also guess how many electoral votes their home state has. Distribute the *Mapping the Electoral College Primary Source Connection* activity sheet (pages 140–141) to students. Confirm students' guesses. Then discuss the map with students. Allow them to work with a partner to answer the questions. Have students discuss their answers in small groups before turning in their answers.

Differentiation Idea

Have **English language learners** work with a **proficient English-speaking** partner. Have them collaborate to identify three states with 20 or more electoral votes and three states with five or fewer electoral votes.

 ## Conduct and Assess

2 Day

1. Have students talk with a partner to review what they learned about the Electoral College system during Day One.

2. Post these fictional popular vote results from the general election in Lesson 8 (page 131): North Corner—Candidate 1 received 8 votes, Candidate 2 received 7 votes; South Corner—Candidate 1 received 7 votes, candidate 2 received 8 votes. Discuss these results as a class. Lead students to understand that as far as the popular vote is concerned, the race seems to be a tie between the two candidates, with 15 votes from each precinct.

Lesson 9: The Electoral College *(cont.)*

3. Divide the classroom into the two regions in which they voted: the North Corner and the South Corner. Assign about 60 percent of students to be North Corner electors. Assign about 40 percent of students to be South Corner electors. Explain that since the North Corner has a greater population, this region receives more electoral votes. Inform the North Corner of the number of electoral votes it has, to match the number of students in this group. The South Corner has fewer people, so this region has fewer electoral votes. Inform the South Corner of the number of electoral votes it has, to match the number of students in this group.

4. Explain that now that the popular votes have been cast, the Electors will cast their votes. First, they must take an oath. Ask the electors to repeat this oath as you read it: "I, _____, as an elector from the great _____ Corner promise to vote for the candidate who has received the majority of votes from the _____ Corner, which I represent. I swear to be a resident of the great classroom of _____ and also a citizen of the United States of America."

5. Once the electors have taken their oath, allow them to cast their votes. This can be done on ballots or by using the simple statement of "I, an elector of the _____ Corner, vote for _____, the candidate who received the majority of votes." Have each elector use the fictional voting results from Step 2 to cast his or her vote.

6. Tally the electoral votes on the board as the electors vote. Create a T-chart, with the North Corner votes on one side and the South Corner votes on the other. Once all of the electors have voted, announce the results. Candidate 1 should win, since the North Corner has more electors and this candidate has won the popular vote in this region.

7. Have students discuss the Electoral College results in small groups. They should discuss how population contributed to the winner of the popular vote versus the electoral vote and think about what this means during a presidential election. (Students should conclude that a presidential candidate can win the election even though he or she did not have the most popular votes.)

8. This may be a good time to do the Election Fun Fact Activity (page 136). It will allow students to see how the Electoral College can affect the outcome of an election.

9. Congratulate the winner of the election. Then, tell students that the inauguration will take place in the next few days.

10. Distribute *The Electoral College Comprehension Check* activity sheet (page 144) to assess students' understanding of the Electoral College system. Use the Comprehension Check Rubric (page 15) to evaluate students' work. See page 14 for ideas on how to use this activity sheet with your students.

Lesson 9: The Electoral College (cont.)

Extension Ideas

✔ Election Fun Fact Activity

To this date, there are only four times in which a president lost the popular vote but won the Electoral College.

- John Quincy Adams won the presidency in 1824 even though Andrew Jackson won the popular vote.

- In 1876, Rutherford B. Hayes won the presidency over Samuel Tilden. Tilden had 247,000 more popular votes than Hayes, but Hayes won the Electoral College by one vote (185–184 votes at that time). This election has often been considered a controversy and a "setup."

- In 1888, Grover Cleveland defeated Benjamin Harrison in the presidential election. Harrison received over 90,000 more popular votes, but Cleveland won the Electoral College with 233 votes. Harrison only received 168 of the electoral votes.

- George W. Bush won the presidency over Al Gore in 2000. This was the closest presidential election in history. The state of Florida, with 25 electoral votes, gave Bush the presidency.

Have students choose one of these events in history and further research it. Then, they need to create a newspaper article explaining how it happened, why it happened, and the effects of it happening. The article should explain the public response and include pictures or photographs the students have drawn or gotten from the Internet.

Differentiation Idea

As an extension, allow **above-level** students to research the election between Hayes and Tilden. Have them create news reports explaining whether or not it was a "setup."

✔ Research Extension

Students can research the number of electoral votes each state received in earlier elections, such as those in the 1800s. Then, create a map showing these votes. Students then compare the map to the electoral votes candidates receive today and answer the following questions under the map: How have the numbers changed? How many electoral votes were needed to win on the older map? Do you think it was easier to win an election with fewer states, and therefore fewer electoral votes? Why or why not?

✔ Connecting Elections

The Electoral College is only used with the presidential elections. Ask students why they think the framers of the Constitution did not feel it was necessary to have an Electoral College for senators and representatives. Also, ask students if they feel that an Electoral College could work for senators and representatives. Have students give reasons for their answers.

Name: _____ Date: _____

The Electoral College Content-Area Vocabulary

Directions: Read the definitions for each word in the box below. Think about how each word compares to something else. Use the words in the Idea Box or think of some on your own and make a comparison for each word.

Example: The <u>Electoral College</u> is like a <u>baseball game</u> because you never know which team is going to win until the very last at-bat.

---

elector—a citizen chosen to vote in the Electoral College for the president and vice president of the United States

Electoral College—the body of electors who formally elect the United States president and vice president

pledge—a promise; guarantee

popular vote—the votes cast by the public or citizens of a nation

---

Idea Box

| gumball | fire cracker | basketball team | fishing trip | bus ride |
| envelope | camera | video game | phone call | pizza |

---

1. An elector is like a(n) _____ because _____

_____ .

2. The Electoral College is like a(n) _____ because _____

_____ .

3. A pledge is like a(n) _____ because _____

_____ .

4. The popular vote is like a(n) _____ because _____

_____ .

Name: _____ Date: _____

The Electoral College Background Information

Directions: Read the information below.

When voters go to the polls in November to vote for a president, they are really voting for **electors**. These electors **pledge** to vote for certain candidates on the ballot. The number of electors in each state differs. The electors are the same number as the senators and representatives from each state. There are two senators from each state. But the number of representatives is based on a state's population. However, the District of Columbia, though not a state, gets three electors. The minimum number of electoral votes per state is three.

In most of the states, the winner takes all of the electors. Whichever candidate gets the most votes in that state gets all of the electors. So, if a candidate wins Texas, he or she gets all of the electoral votes from Texas.

The **Electoral College** then votes for the president and vice president. Each elector casts one vote. These votes are called *electoral votes*. All electors pledge to be honest and vote for the candidate for whom they promised to vote.

The Electoral College votes in December. The electors meet in their state capitols and cast their votes. The votes are then sent to Washington, DC. On January 6, the votes are counted in Congress.

The candidate that receives the majority of the electoral votes is elected president. It takes 270 electoral votes to win the presidential election. If there is no winner in the Electoral College, then the House of Representatives chooses the president. Four presidents have won the Electoral College even though they did not win the popular vote.

The Electoral College was created in the Constitution. Some of the writers wanted Congress to elect the president. Others wanted the president to be chosen by the **popular vote**. The writers felt the Electoral College would be a compromise between the two ideas. The writers of the Constitution did not think the average citizens were smart enough to choose a president. So, they created electors. These electors were the educated upper class, and they had the final vote.

Many people do not like the Electoral College. However, it would not be easy to remove it from the election process. An amendment would have to be added to the Constitution. In order for that to happen, two-thirds of the House would have to approve the amendment. Then it would go to the Senate. Two-thirds of the Senate would also have to approve it. Finally, it would go to the voters. Three-fourths of all states would have to approve the amendment as well. That would be all but 13 states. There have been over 700 proposed amendments to get rid of the Electoral College, but all of them have failed.

Name: _____ Date: _____

The Electoral College

Directions: Use information from *The Electoral College Background Information* activity sheet. Draw a picture to show how the Electoral College decides the winner of a presidential election. Be sure to also show the popular vote in your drawing. Answer the questions.

1. Why is the Electoral College system part of the Constitution?

_____

_____

_____

2. Why is the Electoral College system still part of the process to elect a president even though some people do not like it?

_____

_____

_____

Name: _____ Date: _____

Mapping the Electoral College Primary Source Connection

Directions: Read the information below.

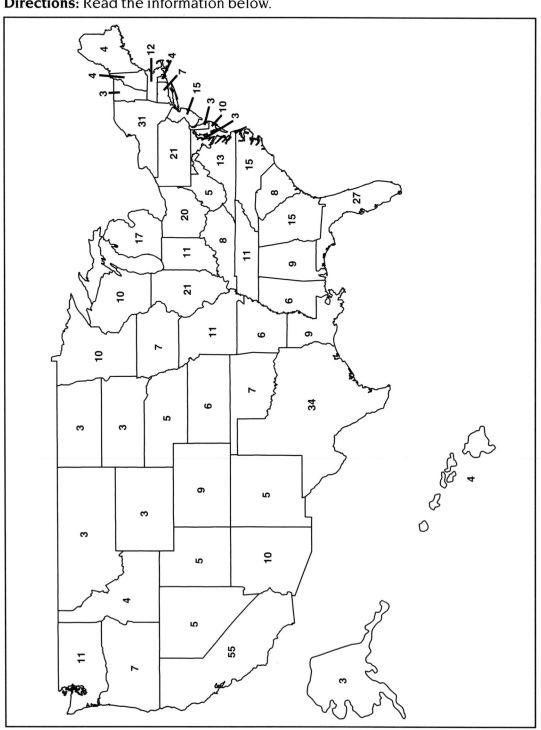

Primary Source Background Information

This map shows the electoral votes projected for the 2008 elections. It states the number of electors each state has. There are a total of 538 electors, with a candidate needing 270 electoral votes to win.

Mapping the Electoral College Primary Source Connection *(cont.)*

Primary Source Questions

1. Which state has the most electoral votes? How many electoral votes does it get? Why does it have the most votes?

_____

_____

_____

_____

2. Which five states do you think are most important to the candidates? Why?

_____

_____

_____

_____

3. How can the states with fewer electoral votes affect an election?

_____

_____

_____

_____

Primary Source Extension

If you were in government, would you try to change the Electoral College? What plan would you develop to make it easier and/or better? On a separate sheet of paper, propose your own amendment that would allow the elections to be fair. Would you keep the Electoral College but reform it? Or, would you try to get rid of it completely? Explain all of your ideas in the proposed amendment.

Name: _____ Date: _____

The Electoral College vs. the Popular Vote

Directions: Is the Electoral College necessary? Or, should the popular vote be the final vote? Write at least five arguments for each idea under the headings below. Then, complete the writing assignment on the following page.

Supporting the Electoral College	Supporting the Popular Vote

The Electoral College vs. the Popular Vote *(cont.)*

Writing Assignment

Directions: Decide which idea you have the stronger argument for. Write a paragraph that convinces government leaders to either keep or get rid of the Electoral College.

- State your opinion at the beginning of the paragraph.
- Include at least three reasons to support your opinion.
- Restate your opinion in a different way when concluding the paragraph.

_____

_____

_____

_____

_____

_____

_____

_____

_____

_____

_____

_____

_____

_____

_____

_____

Name: _____ Date: _____

The Electoral College Comprehension Check

Directions: On a separate sheet of paper, answer the questions below according to the directions from your teacher.

★ Remember

Write three words that are related to the Electoral College. Include their meanings.

★ Understand

Explain how a presidential candidate can win the election, even if he or she does not win the popular vote. Write your answer in paragraph form.

★ Apply

What questions would you ask a Founding Father about the Electoral College? List those questions. Then, write answers they might give to the questions.

★ Analyze

Which is more important: the Electoral College or the popular vote? Decide by creating a T-chart that shows the pros and cons of both.

★ Evaluate

Plan a debate with a partner. Your partner will state reasons to eliminate the Electoral College system. Write two reasons your debate partner might use to explain why he or she wants to eliminate it. You are to defend the Electoral College, stating why it is necessary. Write one counterreason to support the Electoral College system for each of your debate partner's reasons to eliminate it.

★ Create

Create an unusual way to show the process of the Electoral College to your classmates. You might draw a picture of a machine showing how the voting system works. You might make a model of the system, using common items such as paper clips to act as the votes.

Lesson 10: Inauguration Day

Standard

- Students will understand why becoming knowledgeable about public affairs, such as Inauguration Day, is a form of political participation (McREL Civics 28.6)

Vocabulary

- address
- ball
- Capitol
- inauguration
- oath

Materials

- *Inauguration Day Content-Area Vocabulary* (page 150)
- *Taking the Oath Background Information* (page 151)
- *Taking the Oath* (page 152)
- *A Day to Remember Primary Source Connection* (pages 153–154)
- *A Night at the Ball* (page 155)
- *Inauguration Day Comprehension Check* (page 156)
- Food and supplies for Inauguration Day (*optional*)

Introduce the Content

Teacher Preparation: Set a reasonable future date for the class to have its own Inauguration Day.

1. If you have not completed the previous lessons, review with students the steps that lead to a president getting inaugurated.

2. Display a picture of the Capitol building in Washington, DC. Asks students to predict the significance of this building as it relates to elections. Distribute the *Inauguration Day Content-Area Vocabulary* activity sheet (page 150) to students. Review the definitions as a class and allow students to complete this page independently or with a partner. You may also ask students to complete a Vocabulary Extension Activity.

Differentiation Idea

Work with **English language learners** in a small group to complete the vocabulary page. If possible, provide pictures of each term or talk about the terms and what examples might look like. Support their efforts to write one complete sentence for each term.

Lesson 10: Inauguration Day *(cont.)*

✔ Vocabulary Extension Activities

- Ask students to use at least three of the vocabulary words to create their own inaugural address.

- Have students think about how the presidential candidates feel on Inauguration Day. Then, have them create diary entries that express these feelings. Students should use at least three of the vocabulary words in their diary entries.

3. Distribute copies of *Taking the Oath Background Information* (page 151) and *Taking the Oath* (page 152) activity sheets. Read the information to the class as they follow along. Then discuss with students what Inauguration Day entails. Write an outline on the board, based on the background information. Have students complete the activity sheet, comparing early and present-day inaugurations independently or with a partner.

4. Distribute *A Day to Remember Primary Source Connection* activity sheet (pages 153–154) to students. Have students work with a partner. They should take turns reading the speeches aloud to each other. Discuss as a class what information was included in the speeches. Finally, ask students to answer the questions with their partner. Students who do not finish this sheet may complete it as homework.

 **Begin the Activity**

1. Again, display a picture of the Capitol building. Ask a volunteer to explain its significance with regard to elections. (This is where the newly elected president takes the Oath of Office and gives his or her inaugural address.)

2. Display the current Oath of Office and read it to the class. Discuss the Oath of Office as a class and summarize what the newly elected president promises to do. Divide students into small groups. Have them write an oath for the newly elected class president to take on Inauguration Day (Day Three of this lesson). Once all the groups have finished, have each group share their oaths aloud with the class. Compare ideas common to all the groups included. Then, write a class oath for Inauguration Day. Include the common ideas from all the groups in the class oath.

> **Article II of U.S. Constitution, Section 1**
> Before he enters on the execution of this office, he shall take the following oath or affirmation:
> "I do solemnly swear (or affirm) I will faithfully execute the Office of President of the United States, and will to the best of my Ability, preserve, protect, and defend the Constitution of the United States."

Lesson 10: Inauguration Day (cont.)

Differentiation Idea

Allow **English language learners** to record their oaths using a tape recorder. This way, they can speak rather than write their ideas. Provide examples of oaths so that students can completely understand what oaths are.

3. Have students reflect on the excerpts of inaugural addresses from the Primary Source sheet from Day One (e.g., unity and hope). Discuss with students why presidents give speeches at their inaugurations. Then ask what they think the classroom president's inaugural speech should entail. Write their ideas on the board.

4. Explain that the class will have its own Inauguration Day on _____ (share date with the class). Divide the class into small groups. Then, distribute copies of A *Night at the Ball* activity sheet (page 155) to students. Challenge students to brainstorm in their groups possible events that could take place during the inauguration of the new class president. Encourage students to be creative as they plan events.

5. Give students time to plan the day's events. You may also wish to send notes home to parents about three to five days prior to the event to allow them time to prepare or purchase any food for the party, if necessary.

6. Allow students to share their ideas with the class as you write them on the board. Decide on one theme as a class. Then, create a class schedule for Inauguration Day events.

7. Assign different students different tasks related to the events on Inauguration Day, depending on the activities they included on the class schedule. The newly elected president and vice president should write inaugural speeches based on the class suggestions (see Step 3). Other students should be assigned activities, such as writing speeches, planning the ball, and writing poetry and music.

Differentiation Idea

Allow **English language learners** and **lower-level students** to choose the activities they wish to complete for the inauguration.

Lesson 10: Inauguration Day *(cont.)*

Conclude and Assess

1. Begin Inauguration Day by telling students that you will act as the Chief Justice of the Supreme Court. You will be giving the Oath of Office for the president and vice president.

2. Following the outline of events created by the class on Day Two, ask the president and vice president to come forward. Then have them take the oaths of office written by the class.

3. Follow the remaining timeline of events to complete the rest of the day's activities, including the Inaugural Ball.

4. Distribute the *Inauguration Day Comprehension Check* activity sheet (page 156) to assess students' understanding of the president's inauguration. Use the Comprehension Check Rubric (page 15) to evaluate students' work. See page 14 for ideas on how to use this activity sheet with your students.

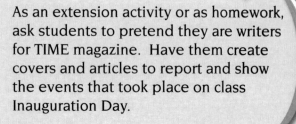

Differentiation Idea

As an extension activity or as homework, ask students to pretend they are writers for TIME magazine. Have them create covers and articles to report and show the events that took place on class Inauguration Day.

Extension Ideas

✔ Election Fun Fact Activity

Read the fun facts below. Then, have students complete the activity that follows.

Presidents spend varying amounts of money on their inaugurations.

- Jimmy Carter claimed to be a "people's president." Therefore, he spent only $3.5 million on his inauguration, which was considered a small amount. He also set the limit for his inaugural ball tickets at $25. After he was sworn in on Capitol Hill, he walked back to the White House rather than ride in a limousine.

- Ronald Reagan spent $16 million on his inauguration. And, he charged up to $1,000 for his inaugural ball tickets.

- George H. W. Bush attended 11 inaugural balls, a high for that time period. But the Clintons topped that by attending 14 balls when Bill Clinton was inaugurated in 1997.

- Thomas Jefferson held no party. He walked to the Capitol for his oath. Afterward, he went back to his house to rest.

- Though George Washington received a party after he was inaugurated, the tradition of inaugural balls did not begin until the election of James Madison in 1809. Tickets for this ball cost $4.

Create a program to show what you would do at your ball and inauguration, the price you would charge, and what it would entail. Would it be fancy? Or, would you prefer something similar to that of Jimmy Carter or Thomas Jefferson? Explain the events in your evening's (or afternoon's) program.

 Lesson 10: Inauguration Day *(cont.)*

Research Extension

Either assign each student a president or have each student choose a president. Ask students to research the inaugural address of the president they have chosen. Have each student choose one portion of the addresses to summarize. In their summaries, students should explain what the speeches stated and how it may have affected those listening. Ask students to include pictures of the inaugurations, if possible.

Connecting Elections

The Constitution only gives an oath of office to the president. Senators, representatives, and the vice president do not have set oaths. However, the following oath has been taken since 1884 by those holding these offices:

"I do solemnly swear (or affirm) that I will support and defend the Constitution of the United States against all enemies, foreign and domestic; that I will bear true faith and allegiance to the same; that I take this obligation freely, without any mental reservation or purpose of evasion; and that I will well and faithfully discharge the duties of the office on which I am about to enter. So help me God."

Share the above facts with the students. Then, ask each student to answer the following: Why do you suppose writers of the Constitution did not create an oath for other offices in the government? Pretend you are a writer of the Constitution. Explain your reasoning for only creating an oath for the president.

Name: _____ Date: _____

Inauguration Day Content-Area Vocabulary

Directions: Use the definitions below to illustrate each vocabulary word. Write a sentence with the term to explain your picture.

address—a speech given by an elected official at the inauguration

ball—a party given after the winning candidate is inaugurated into office

Capitol—the main building of the United States Congress (the Senate and the House of Representatives)

inauguration—the act of starting or being inducted into a new position

oath—a formal or legal pledge or promise

Vocabulary Word	Illustration	Sentence
address		
ball		
Capitol		
inauguration		
oath		

Name: _____ Date: _____

Taking the Oath Background Information

Directions: Read the information below.

The final step of the election process is the **inauguration**. This is the start of the new president's term in office. It takes place on January 20, after the general election. The inauguration used to take place in March. Many years ago, it took more time to collect election results. Then, the winning candidate had to travel to Washington, DC. The 20th Amendment came into effect in 1930. It changed the inaugural date to January 20.

The first presidents were inaugurated in a few different cities. George Washington was inaugurated in both New York City and Philadelphia. John Adams was inaugurated in Philadelphia, too. Thomas Jefferson was the first to be inaugurated in Washington, DC. Today, the inauguration always occurs in Washington, DC. It takes place somewhere near the United States **Capitol** building.

The inauguration marks the end of one presidential term and the beginning of another. It makes the transition official. Inauguration Day involves the public. People gather to see this major event. Members of all political parties attend.

Inauguration Day is a time of celebration. First, the president and vice president take the **Oaths** of Office. The Chief Justice of the U.S. Supreme Court leads the president in the Oath. The Oath is written in the Constitution. The new president then gives an inaugural **address**. This is a special speech. It often reminds supporters why the president was elected. The new president

also states promises for the next four years. Prayers are often said, and poetry is read. Music is played, and parades can be held. The day ends with many different inaugural **balls**. Anyone who has purchased tickets may attend.

This is an invitation to Abraham Lincoln's inaugural ball on March 4, 1865.

Name: _____ Date: _____

Taking the Oath

Directions: Use details from *Taking the Oath Background Information* activity sheet. Compare how early presidential inaugurations are different from present-day inaugurations.

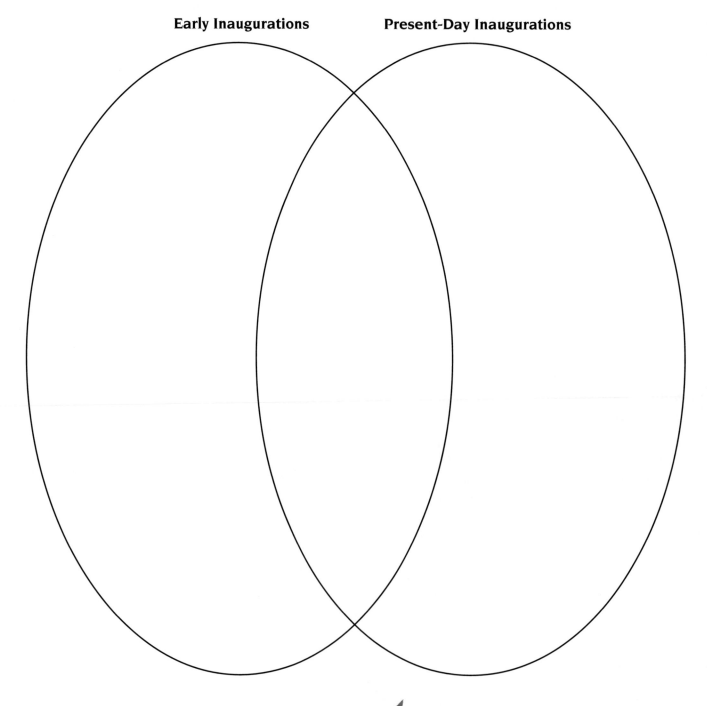

Early Inaugurations   Present-Day Inaugurations

Name: _____   Date: _____

A Day to Remember Primary Source Connection

Directions: Read the information below.

Excerpts from Inauguration Speeches

"With malice toward none; with charity for all; with firmness in the right, as God gives us to see the right, let us strive on to finish the work we are in; to bind up the nation's wounds; to care for him who shall have borne the battle, and for his widow, and his orphan—to do all which may achieve and cherish a just and lasting peace, among ourselves, and with all nations."

—*Abraham Lincoln, March 4, 1865*

"I am certain that my fellow Americans expect that on my induction into the Presidency I will address them with a candor and a decision which the present situation of our Nation impels. This is preeminently the time to speak the truth, the whole truth, frankly and boldly. Nor need we shrink from honestly facing conditions in our country today. This great Nation will endure as it has endured, will revive and will prosper. So, first of all, let me assert my firm belief that the only thing we have to fear is fear itself—nameless, unreasoning, unjustified terror which paralyzes needed efforts to convert retreat into advance. In every dark hour of our national life a leadership of frankness and vigor has met with that understanding and support of the people themselves which is essential to victory. I am convinced that you will again give that support to leadership in these critical days."

—*Franklin D. Roosevelt, Saturday, March 4, 1933*

"And so, my fellow Americans: ask not what your country can do for you—ask what you can do for your country. My fellow citizens of the world: ask not what America will do for you, but what together we can do for the freedom of man. Finally, whether you are citizens of America or citizens of the world, ask of us the same high standards of strength and sacrifice which we ask of you. With a good conscience our only sure reward, with history the final judge of our deeds, let us go forth to lead the land we love, asking His blessing and His help, but knowing that here on earth God's work must truly be our own."

—*John F. Kennedy, Friday, January 20, 1961*

Primary Source Background Information

The excerpts above are from inaugural addresses delivered by some of our most famous presidents: Abraham Lincoln, Franklin D. Roosevelt, and John F. Kennedy.

A Day to Remember Primary Source Connection *(cont.)*

Primary Source Questions

1. Compare two of the speeches by stating at least three similarities.

_____

_____

_____

_____

2. What major event was happening in the United States during Roosevelt's election? What words does he use to give hope to the country during this crisis?

_____

_____

_____

_____

3. The three speeches give hope for the future. Choose quotations from two of the speeches that encourage the citizens to be hopeful. Explain how each quotation shows hope.

_____

_____

_____

_____

_____

Primary Source Extension

If you were a speechwriter for the next president, what would you say about our nation? What hope would you give for the future? What would you discuss in the inauguration speech? On a separate sheet of paper, write an inaugural address for the next president based on the history of our nation today.

Name: _____ Date: _____

A Night at the Ball

Directions: Plan events for the inauguration ceremony and the inaugural ball of your newly elected class president.

Theme: _____

Music Suggestions

_____

_____

_____

Food Suggestions

_____

_____

_____

Drink Suggestions

_____

_____

_____

Event Suggestions

_____

_____

_____

Attire (Clothing) Suggestions

_____

_____

_____

Name: _____ Date: _____

Inauguration Day Comprehension Check

Directions: On a separate sheet of paper, answer the questions below according to the directions from your teacher.

★ Remember

List the date present-day inaugurations take place. Explain why every inauguration now takes place on this date.

★ Understand

Explain how today's inaugurations compare to early inaugurations. Include two or more differences and two or more similarities.

★ Apply

Create an invitation that explains the events that take place during an inauguration.

★ Analyze

Presidential inaugurations tend to cost a lot of money—millions of dollars! Think about the events that take place during an inauguration. List the top three events you think cost the most and explain why they made the top of your list.

★ Evaluate

Is the presidential oath sufficient? Why or why not? Write a letter to Congress stating your opinion and ways in which you would change the oath or stating why you would not change it.

★ Create

Create a mural of "snapshots" showing inaugural events. Then create captions for the pictures in your mural. Your snapshots can be photographs, drawings, clip art, or pictures from magazines.

Answer Key

Party Time Graphic Organizer (page 23)

Democrats—Beliefs: keep our nation safe, expand opportunities for every American, affordable health care for all Americans, improving Social Security, honest government and civil rights; **History:** oldest, began as the Democratic-Republican Party, created by Thomas Jefferson in 1792; **Symbol:** donkey

Republicans—Beliefs: keep our nation safe, strength lies with individuals; honor each person's dignity, freedom, ability, and responsibility; government should be responsible with money; let workers keep money; government provides services others cannot, extend peace, freedom, and human rights throughout the world; **History:** formed in 1854 by people who opposed the Kansas-Nebraska Bill, did not want slavery to move to new states, Abraham Lincoln was the first Republican president, called the GOP or Grand Old Party; **Symbol:** elephant

Analyzing Political Parties of the Past (page 25)

1. There are over 50 all together, which is too many to list on one page.
2. The Anti-Monopoly Party only existed in 1884. Student justifications will vary.
3. Democratic, Republican
4. Answers will vary.
5. Answers will vary.

Political Parties Primary Source Connection (pages 26–27)

1. students' answers will vary.
2. Answers will vary, but students may discuss how the elephant appears to be strong in this photograph, which would make it a good symbol.

Political Parties Comprehension Check (page 28)

Answers will vary.

National Elections Content-Area Vocabulary (page 33)

1. candidate
2. Constitution
3. amendment
4. elected
5. representative
6. election

Electing Our Leaders Graphic Organizer (page 35)

Answers will vary.

The Constitution Rules Primary Source Connection (pages 36– 37)

1. Members of the House and Senate were first chosen by electors from the state legislatures. They are now chosen in general elections.
2. The Constitution allowed one representative for every 30,000 people. There is now a maximum of 435. Answers will vary, but may include that the growth of the population could mean an extremely large number of representatives.
3. Senators are divided into three classes to determine elections.
4. The vice president can affect the outcome of a bill because he or she gets the deciding vote if there is a tie, thereby possibly affecting if a bill passes or fails in the Senate.

National Elections Comprehension Check (page 38)

Answers will vary.

State and Local Elections Content-Area Vocabulary (page 43)

1. government
2. legislation
3. governor
4. vacancy
5. appoint
6. governor; appoint
7. government
8. vacancy
9. governor; legislation

Electing State and Local Officials (page 45)

Governor—What He or She Does: leads the state, vetoes bills, appoints senators if there is a vacancy; **Qualifications:** differ from state to state; most must be citizens of the United States; there is an age requirement; most must have been residents of their state for a certain number of years; **Length of Term:** two or four years; **Who Elects Them:** citizens of that state; **Other Facts:** may be able to serve an unlimited number of terms

Answer Key *(cont.)*

Electing State and Local Officials (page 45) *(cont.)*

Mayor—What He or She Does: leads the city, heads the city council; **Qualifications:** differ from state to state; age requirement; citizen of the United States; resident of that city or state for a certain length of time; **Length of Term:** varies per city (mostly two years); **Who Elects Them:** citizens of that city; **Other Facts:** (none listed)

1. Answers will vary. Students should explain the importance of the governor.
2. Answers will vary. Students should explain the importance of the mayor.

Climbing the Political Ladder (pages 49–50)

Students' answers will vary.

1. Students should state the similarities among the three offices.
2. Students should explain why the qualifications were or were not what they expected.
3. Students should give reasons as to why they find the qualifications either fair or unfair.

Milking the Governor's Cow Primary Source Connection (pages 51–52)

1. At this time, when the Union was unstable, the governor was trying to get more states to secede from the Union. If he were successful, then what became the Confederacy would be even stronger.
2. "Governor, if you pull too hard on my tail, I will kick you into the Atlantic Ocean." This may mean that the Union will fight to stay together.
3. "I have a good constitution and can stand a pretty strong pull." Having a good Constitution helps the government stay strong and united.

State and Local Elections Comprehension Check (page 53)

Answers will vary.

Running for President Content-Area Vocabulary (page 59)

Students' personal definitions and examples will vary.

In the Running Graphic Organizer (page 61)

1. answer provided
2. announce running or give a speech to announce running
3. qualify to run
4. gain delegate support
5. delegates vote at the national convention
6. answer provided

Running the Race Primary Source Connection (pages 62–63)

1. This cartoon tells who the candidates are and how they are doing in the race.
2. Webster ran as an independent.
3. Answers will vary.

Running for Class President (page 64)

Answers will vary.

Running for President Comprehension Check (page 65)

Answers will vary.

The Primaries Content-Area Vocabulary (page 71)

1. primary election
2. open primary
3. closed primary
4. presidential primary
5. runoff primary
6. caucus
7. Only members from a particular party can vote for candidates of the same party in a closed primary. Anyone can vote for any candidate in an open primary.
8. Answers will vary.
9. It is more like a meeting than an election.
10. Both require deciding on nominees.

Answer Key (cont.)

The Primaries Purpose Graphic Organizer (pages 73–74)

1. Students should give their opinions as to the best type of primary, based on their lists. They should give reasons to support their opinions.
2. Each student should list his or her strongest point for closed primaries.
3. Each student should list his or her strongest point for open primaries.
4. Students should state the type of primary they would choose, giving reasons for their answers.
5. Students should give reasons as to why they think politicians may prefer one primary over the other. Reasons for a closed primary may include that there can be no raiding; for an open primary: "It gives everyone the chance to vote for any party, rather than having to declare a party."

The Primary Vote Primary Source Connection (pages 75–76)

1. Matt Gaetz; 42.5%
2. Jose Oliva; 42.0%
3. One year
4. The 2010 election had more candidates.
5. They are also similar because the winners both received approximately 42% of the votes.
6. Students should say whether they think voter turnout was high, low, or if they cannot tell and support their answer.

The Primaries Comprehension Check (page 79)

Answers will vary.

The National Convention Content-Area Vocabulary (page 85)

1. party platform; Student examples and nonexamples will vary.
2. committee; Student examples and nonexamples will vary.
3. legitimate; Student examples and nonexamples will vary.
4. majority; Student examples and nonexamples will vary.

A Night to Remember Graphic Organizer (page 87)

Who: committees, delegates, nominees, keynote speaker, chairman

What: a party with songs, posters, and the selection of a presidential and vice-presidential nominee

Where: city in United States of committee's choosing

When: summer before an election; lasts four days

Why: to nominate a party candidate for president and vice president

How: careful planning by the convention committee

Celebration Night Primary Source Connectio (pages 88–89)

1. National conventions have somewhat of a party atmosphere with balloons, hats, and buttons being worn. People seem to be smiling and laughing.
2. Present in the pictures are the delegates, the presidential candidate and his wife, and the vice-presidential candidate and his wife.
3. Answers will vary, but may include to unify a party, to come together and officially announce the president and vice president, and to show support for the presidential nominee.
4. Answers will vary, but may include that the presidential and vice-presidential nominees unite with hands held and raised, the party platforms are created, and support is shown through posters, songs, and keynote speeches.

Planning the Party (page 90)

Answers will vary.

The National Convention Comprehension Check (page 92)

Answers will vary.

The Race Is On! Content Area Vocabulary (page 101)

1. endorse
2. campaign
3. propaganda
4. media
5. lobbyist
6. debate

Students' illustrations will vary.

Answer Key *(cont.)*

Hot on the Trail Graphic Organizer (page 104)

1828: Andrew Jackson; used buttons and banners showing his military experience

1840: William Henry Harrison and John Tyler; first campaign slogan, "Tippecanoe and Tyler, too"; slogan used in buttons, banners, and songs; candidates toured the nation; gave speeches and explained their policies

1858: Stephen A. Douglas and Abraham Lincoln; first debates; held outside in seven cities in Illinois; crowds cheered and booed; debates printed in newspapers

1960: John F. Kennedy and Richard M. Nixon; first televised debates; held four debates that millions of voters watched or listened to them on the radio

1. Jackson used buttons and banners whereas Harrison and Tyler's slogan was used in songs and they also toured the nation, giving speeches.
2. Kennedy's campaign was televised whereas Lincoln's campaign was printed in newspapers.
3. Answers will vary.
4. Answers will vary.

Campaigning with Posters Primary Source Connection (pages 105–106)

1. The Lincoln poster items that stand out include the eagle, the two statues of Justice and Liberty, the American flags, and the paper at the bottom that reads "The Union." The Carter poster items that stand out include the large smile on the peanut and the peanut itself.
2. Answers might include that the Lincoln poster seems to be more serious, showing more of his beliefs about liberty, justice, and the union, while the Carter poster is a bit sillier, showing possibly more of his personality with the large smile shown on the poster.
3. Answers will vary, but students may argue that the Carter poster does not really show what he stands for. The Lincoln poster does a better job by stating the beliefs of Abraham Lincoln.
4. Lincoln's poster shows us that he wants justice, unity, and liberty. Carter's poster doesn't really show us his beliefs or positions. Based on this answer, students may conclude that the Lincoln poster tells us more about the candidate.

Account Tracking Task Sheet (page 108)

Answers will vary.

Pollster Polls Task Sheet (page 113)

Answers will vary.

Campaign Manager Responsibilities Task Sheet (page 114)

Answers will vary.

The Race Is On! Comprehension Check (page 115)

Answers will vary.

The Vote Is In! Content-Area Vocabulary (page 121)

Answers will vary.

Rocking the Vote Graphic Organizer (page 123)

15th Amendment: 1870; after the Civil War; citizens of all races and all colors; voting could no longer be denied on the grounds of race or color

19th Amendment: 1920; women; citizens could not be denied the right to vote based on whether they were men or women

26th Amendment: after the Vietnam War; anyone ages 18 to 20; changed the voting age from 21 to 18

Counting the Vote Primary Source Connection (pages 124–125)

1. One person appears to be reading a list on a piece of paper that gives the votes that were received, while two other officials appear to be recording the votes.
2. The votes were placed in a wooden box.
3. Some of the people standing around appear to be military officials. Others are members of the United States government, as shown on the sashes of their clothing. Some may just be onlookers.
4. It is different because most of the machines count the ballot, rather than ballots being counted by hand. It is similar because some ballots are still placed in locked boxes.

Answer Key *(cont.)*

Every Vote Counts (pages 129–130)

Possible Pros for Hand Counting: can make sure no votes get skipped, can double-check votes

Possible Cons for Hand Counting: takes longer, human error

Possible Pros for Machine Counting: takes less time, less chance of error

Possible Cons for Machine Counting: may not read votes correctly

1. Students should state the best argument for counting by machines.
2. Students should state the best argument for counting by hand.
3. Students should give reasons based on their lists as to why they feel one technique is better than the other.

The Vote Is In! Comprehension Check (page 132)

Answers will vary.

The Electoral College Content-Area Vocabulary (page 137)

Students' comparisons and reasons will vary.

The Electoral College (page 139)

Students' drawings will vary.

1. Some writers of the Constitution wanted Congress to elect the president. Other writers wanted the president to be chosen by popular vote. The Electoral College is a compromise between the two ideas. The writers of the Constitution did not think the average citizens were smart enough to choose a president. So, they created electors. These electors were the educated upper class, and they had the final vote.
2. The Electoral College system would have to be removed from the election process by Constitutional Amendment. This requires two-thirds vote by the House of Representatives, two-thirds vote by the Senate, and three-fourths vote by the states (about 37 states).

Mapping the Electoral College Primary Source Connection (pages 140–141)

1. California has the most electoral votes. California receives 55 electoral votes because it has the largest population.
2. Answers will vary, but students may say the states with the largest populations because they have the most electoral votes. Some may reason, however, that the states with fewer electoral votes may also be of great importance because they could change the outcome of a close race.
3. States with fewer electoral votes may easily change the outcome of a close race. Even with only three electoral votes, a state might allow a candidate to gain the 270 votes needed to win

The Electoral College vs. the Popular Vote (pages 142–143)

Students' arguments will vary. When grading students' paragraphs, be sure they including the following information:

- The student's opinion was stated at the beginning of the paragraph.
- At least three reasons were given to support the student's opinion.
- The student restated his or her opinion in a different way when concluding the paragraph.

The Electoral College Comprehension Check (page 144)

Answers will vary.

Inauguration Day Content-Area Vocabulary (page 150)

Students' illustrations and sentences will vary.

Taking the Oath Activity Sheet (page 152)

Early Inaugurations: took place in March; took place in different cities

Present-Day Inaugurations: take place on January 20; take place near the Capitol building

Both: ends one term of office and begins another; involves the public; members of all political parties attend; time of celebration; take the Oath written in the Constitution; sworn in by the Chief Justice of the United States Supreme Court; inaugural address is given

Answer Key *(cont.)*

A Day to Remember Primary Source Connection (pages 153–154)

1. Answers may include the following: Both Lincoln's and Roosevelt's speeches were given during a time of turmoil, so both wanted to repair the country. Both Lincoln's and Kennedy's speeches asked Americans to help in some way. All of the speeches gave hope for the future.

2. The Great Depression was occurring in the United States during Roosevelt's election. Students may include the following passage in their responses: This great Nation will endure as it has endured, will revive and will prosper. So, first of all, let me assert my firm belief that the only thing we have to fear is fear itself—nameless, unreasoning, unjustified terror which paralyzes needed efforts to convert retreat into advance.

3. Students should choose a quote from each speech for a total of three quotes. They should then give reasons as to why each of the quotes gives hope.

A Night at the Ball (page 155)

Answers will vary.

Inauguration Day Comprehension Check (page 156)

Answers will vary.

References Cited

Brookbank, D., S. Grover, K. Kullber, and C. Strawser. 1999. *Improving student achievement through organization of students learning.* Chicago: Master's Action Research Project, Saint Xavier University and IRI/Skylight.

Carnegie Corporation of New York and The Center for Information and Research on Civic Learning and Engagement. 2003. The civic mission of schools. http://www.civicmissionofschools.org/campaign/documents/CivicMissionofSchools.pdf (accessed on July 3, 2007).

Center for Civic Education. 1997. *National standards for civics and government.*

Chapman, C., M. J. Nolin, and K. Kline. 1997. *Student interest in national news and its relation to school courses* (NCES 97-970) U.S. Department of Education, National Center for Education Statistics. Washington, DC: U.S. Government Printing Office. http://nces.ed.gov/pubsearch/pubsinfo.asp?pubid=97970 (accessed on July 6, 2007).

Constitutional Rights Foundation. 2000. Fostering civic responsibility through service learning. *Service-Learning Network.* http://www.crf-usa.org/network/net8_1.html (accessed on July 5, 2007).

Hopkins, G. 1998. Why teach current events? *Education World.* http://www.educationworld.com/a_curr/curr084.shtml (accessed on July 6, 2007).

Kirlin, M. 2005. Promising approaches for strengthening civic education. White paper from the California Campaign for the Civic Mission of Schools http://www.cms-ca.org/CMS%20white%20paper%20final.pdf (accessed July 6, 2007).

Lutkus, A., and A. R. Weiss. 2007. *The nation's report card: Civics* 2006 (NCES 2007–476). U.S. Department of Education, National Center for Education Statistics. Washington, D.C.: U.S. Government Printing Office. http://nces.ed.gov/pubsearch/pubsinfo.asp?pubid=2007476 (accessed July 2, 2007).

Marzano, R. J., J. S. Norford, D. E. Paynter, D. J. Pickering, and B. B. Gaddy. 2001. A *handbook for classroom instruction that works.* Alexandria, VA: Association for Supervision & Curriculum Development.

Marzano, R. J., D. J. Pickering, and J. E. Pollock. 2001. *Classroom instruction that works: Research-based strategies for increasing student achievement.* Alexandria, VA: Association for Supervision and Curriculum Development.

National Council for the Social Studies. 1994. *Expectations of excellence: Curriculum standards for social studies.* Washington, DC: NCSS.

National Reading Panel. 2000. *Teaching children to read: An evidence-based assessment of the scientific research literature on reading and its implications for reading instruction.*

Olsen, K. 1995. Science continuum of concepts for grades K–6. Covington, WA: Books for Educators. http://www.nichd.nih.gov/publications/nrp/smallbooks.htm (accessed April 4, 2005).

Quigley, C. N. 2005. The civic mission of the schools: What constitutes an effective civic education? Paper presented at Education for Democracy: The Civic Mission of the Schools, Sacramento, CA.

Sinatra, R. C., J. Stahl-Glemake, and D. N. Berg. 1984. Improving reading comprehension of disabled readers through semantic mapping. *Reading Teaching* 38:22–29.

Stix, A. 2001. *Social studies strategies for active learning.* Huntington Beach, CA: Shell Education.

Additional Resources

The following resources were referenced when writing the background information pages:

Digital History. The presidency of Andrew Jackson. http://www.digitalhistory.uh.edu/database/article_display.cfm?HHID=637

Doherty, E. J. S. and L. C. Evans. 2000. Electing the president: Simulation similes. Chicago: Zephyr Press.

Fact Monster. Election day on Tuesdays? http://www.factmonster.com/spot/electionday1.html

Fair Vote. Past attempts at reform. http://www.fairvote.org/?page=979

Founder's Constitution, The. James Madison, federalist, no. 62, 415-22, article 1, section 3, clauses 1 and 2. http://press-pubs.uchicago.edu/founders/documents/a1_3_1-2s11.html

Franklin and Marshall College. Rendell's raiders. http://www.fandm.edu/x3902.xml.

Hamilton, A., J. Madison, and J. Jay. 1961. *The Federalist*. ed. Jacob E. Cooke. Middletown, CT: Wesleyan University Press.

Harper Week. Cartoon of the Day—The third-term panic. http://www.harpweek.com/09Cartoon/BrowseByDateCartoon.asp?Month=November&Date=7

Horn, G. 2004. *Political parties, interest groups, and the media*. Milwaukee, WI: World Almanac Library.

Johnston, R. D. 2002. *The making of America*. Washington, DC: National Geographic Society.

Joint Congressional Committee of Inaugural Ceremonies. Facts and firsts. http://inaugural.senate.gov/history/factsandfirsts/index.

Library of Congress for Teachers, The. The learning page: Elections… the American way. http://www.loc.gov/teachers/classroommaterials/presentationsandactivities/presentations/elections/home.html

Longley, R. "Why Third Parties?" About.com News & Issues http://usgovinfo.about.com/cs/politicalsystem/a/thirdparties.htm

McGuire, M. E. 1997. *Storypath: The presidential election sourcebook*. Seattle, WA: Everyday Learning Corporation.

Missouri General Assembly. Missouri revised statutes. Chapter 77, third class cities, section 77.230. http://www.moga.mo.gov/statutes/C000-099/0770000230.htm

Project Vote Smart. Government 101: Introduction. http://www.vote-smart.org/resource_govt101_01.php

Safire, W. 1972. "Origin of the elephant." In New language of politics. Rev. ed. New York: Collier Books.

U.S. National Archives and Records Administration. U.S. electoral college. http://www.archives.gov/federal-register/electoral-college

Elections Glossary

address—a speech given by an elected official at the inauguration

advocate—to be in favor of something

amendment—a law or statement added to the Constitution or another document

appoint—to assign or name to a job or duty

ball—a party given after the winning candidate is inaugurated into office

ballot—a sheet of paper or a card used to cast or register a vote, especially a secret one

campaign—an organized effort to achieve a specific goal

candidate—someone who runs for political office

Capitol—the main building of the United States Congress (the Senate and the House of Representatives)

caucus—a meeting held to decide nominees for political parties

citizen—a member of a nation or community by birth or other means

closed primary—an election in which people can only vote for members of their own party

committee—a special group that comes together to work on a matter

conservative—to be resistant to reform or change; avoiding excess

Constitution—laws written to show how the government will be formed

debate—a discussion, usually between two people, in which ideas are given for or against issues

delegates—people appointed to represent others

Democratic Party—the oldest political party in the United States, formed in 1792; one of the two main political parties today

elected—to be selected by voters for an office or position

election—the way voters select winners for political offices

elector—a citizen chosen to vote in the Electoral College for the president and vice president of the United States

Electoral College—the body of electors who formally elect the United States president and vice president

endorse—to approve of; support

general election—the final election in which every eligible citizen can vote for the candidates of his or her choice

government—the system by which a nation or state is run

governor—the leader of a state

inauguration—the act of starting or being inducted into a new position

Elections Glossary *(cont.)*

legislation—the act of making laws

legitimate—to be lawful or legal

liberal—to be broad minded; having political ideas of reform and progress

lobbyist—a person who tries to persuade politicians to vote for bills they support

majority—the greater number; more than half

media—a way to report, write, edit, photograph, or otherwise broadcast news

national convention—an assembly where a candidate is chosen by his or her party to run for president

oath—a formal or legal pledge or promise

open primary—an election in which people can vote for any candidate from any party

party platform—the ideas, goals, and principles of a political party

pledge—a promise; guarantee

political party—an organization or group that shares similar ideas and hopes to gain political offices and power

polling station—a place where voters go to cast their votes during an election

popular vote—the votes cast by the public or citizens of a nation

presidential primary—an election in which nominees are chosen by each party to run for president

primary election—an election in which nominees are chosen to represent the different parties in upcoming elections

propaganda—information that is spread to promote a person or cause

register—to enroll or sign up to vote

representative—a person who represents other people or a specific party

Republican Party—one of the two main political parties today, formed in 1854

right—something that is due to a person or governmental body by law, tradition, or nature

runoff primary—an election held after the primary election to decide on the top two candidates

vacancy—a position that is available for someone to fill

vote—to express one's decision, as in an election

Contents of the Teacher Resource CD

Student Activity Sheets

Page(s)	Title	Filename
21–22	Party Time Background Information	partybackinfo.pdf
23	Party Time Graphic Organizer	partyorganizer.pdf
24	Outlining Political Parties of the Past	politicalpast.pdf
25	Analyzing Political Parties of the Past	analyzeparties.pdf
26–27	Political Parties Primary Source Connection	politicalprimary.pdf
28	Political Parties Comprehension Check	politicalcomp.pdf
33	National Elections Content-Area Vocabulary	electionvocab.pdf
34	Electing Our Leaders Background Information	leaderbackinfo.pdf
35	Electing Our Leaders Graphic Organizer	electorganize.pdf
36–37	The Constitution Rules Primary Source Connection	constitutionprimary.pdf
38	National Elections Comprehension Check	nationalcomp.pdf
43	State and Local Elections Content-Area Vocabulary	statelocalvocab.pdf
44	Our Local Leaders Background Information	localbackinfo.pdf
45	Electing State and Local Officials	electstatelocal.pdf
46–48	State and Local Cards	statelocalcards.pdf
49–50	Climbing the Political Ladder	climbladder.pdf
51–52	Milking the Governor's Cow Primary Source Connection	milkprimary.pdf
53	State and Local Elections Comprehension Check	statelocalcomp.pdf
59	Running for President Content-Area Vocabulary	runvocab.pdf
60	In the Running Background Information	runbackinfo.pdf
61	In the Running Graphic Organizer	runorganizer.pdf
62–63	Running the Race Primary Source Connection	raceprimary.pdf
64	Running for Class President	runpresident.pdf
65	Running for President Comprehension Check	runningcomp.pdf
71	The Primaries Content-Area Vocabulary	primariesvocab.pdf
72	The Primary Purpose Background Information	primarybackinfo.pdf
73–74	The Primary Purpose Graphic Organizer	primaryorganizer.pdf
75–76	The Primary Vote Primary Source Connection	voteprimary.pdf
77	Newsbreak! Simulation Cards	newsbreakcards.pdf
78	Primary Voting Ballots	votingballots.pdf
79	The Primaries Comprehension Check	primariescomp.pdf
85	The National Convention Content-Area Vocabulary	nationalvocab.pdf
86	A Night to Remember Background Information	nightbackinfo.pdf
87	A Night to Remember Graphic Organizer	nightorganizer.pdf
88–89	Celebration Night Primary Source Connection	celebrationprimary.pdf

Contents of the Teacher Resource CD *(cont.)*

Student Activity Sheets *(cont.)*

Page(s)	Title	Filename
90–91	Planning the Party	planparty.pdf
92	The National Convention Comprehension Check	conventioncomp.pdf
101	The Race is On! Content-Area Vocabulary	racevocab.pdf
102–103	Hot on the Trail Background Information	trailbackinfo.pdf
104	Hot on the Trail Graphic Organizer	trailorganizer.pdf
105–106	Campaigning with Posters Primary Source Connection	campaignprimary.pdf
107	Joining the Campaign Job Cards	jobcards.pdf
108	Account Tracking Task Sheet	trackingsheet.pdf
109	Advertising Staff Cost List of Campaign Materials Task Sheet	campaigntask.pdf
110–111	Debate Outline Task Sheet	debateoutline.pdf
112	Press Secretary Situation Cards Task Sheet	presscardstask.pdf
113	Pollster Polls Task Sheet	pollstertasksheet.pdf
114	Campaign Manager Responsibilities Task Sheet	managertasksheet.pdf
115	The Race Is On! Comprehension Check	racecomp.pdf
121	The Vote Is In! Content-Area Vocabulary	votevocab.pdf
122	Rocking the Vote Background Information	rockbackinfo.pdf
123	Rocking the Vote Graphic Organizer	rockorganizer.pdf
124–125	Counting the Vote Primary Source Connection	countingprimary.pdf
126	Voter Registration Cards	registrationcards.pdf
127	Voter Sign-In Sheet	votersheet.pdf
128	Voting Ballots	votingballots.pdf
129–130	Every Vote Counts	votecounts.pdf
131	Voting Results News Flashes	voteresults.pdf
132	The Vote Is In! Comprehension Check	voteisincomp.pdf
137	The Electoral College Content-Area Vocabulary	electoralvocab.pdf
138	The Electoral College Background Information	politicalbackinfo.pdf
139	The Electoral College	electoralcollege.pdf
140–141	Mapping the Electoral College Primary Source Connection	mapprimary.pdf
142–143	The Electoral College vs. the Popular Vote	electoralvspop.pdf
144	The Electoral College Comprehension Check	electoralcomp.pdf
150	Inauguration Day Content-Area Vocabulary	inaugurationvocab.pdf
151	Taking the Oath Background Information	oathbackinfo.pdf
152	Taking the Oath	oathactivity.pdf
153–154	A Day to Remember Primary Source Connection	dayprimary.pdf
155	A Night at the Ball	nightball.pdf
156	Inauguration Day Comprehension Check	inaugurationcomp.pdf